A HISTORY of EUROPE

A HISTORY of EUROPE

From pre-history to the 21st century

Jeremy Black

This edition published in 2021 by Arcturus Publishing Limited
26/27 Bickels Yard, 151–153 Bermondsey Street,
London SE1 3HA

AD007740UK

Printed in the UK

CONTENTS

INTRODUCTION

Europe is a compact continent with a fascinating history, one that is important both for those who live there today and for the rest of the world. The expansion of the European powers – of Russia to the Pacific and into Central Asia, and of Britain, France, Belgium, Denmark, the Netherlands, Germany, Italy, Portugal and Spain across the oceans – repeatedly affected, indeed transformed, the history of the world from the 15th century to the present. It is understandable that many focus their attention on these recent centuries, but the deep history of Europe and its peoples, and their millennia of development, was also extremely important for what came later, both for Europe and the rest of the world, and it remains significant to the present.

WHERE IS EUROPE?

Europe as understood in this book is a geographical concept, an area located between Asia and the Atlantic. But this approach is open to debate. For example, although the Ural mountains have conventionally been seen as the eastern physical border of Europe, they are neither a barrier nor a frontier, being located from 1917 in the Russian Soviet Federative Socialist Republic, and from December 1991 in the Russian Federation.

Europe is different to other continents. It has a longer coastline relative to its size than other continents, and is very much the maritime continent. Its climate is subject to the interplay of an oceanic source of low pressure and a Eurasian source of high pressure, and of cold winds from the Arctic and hot winds from the Sahara, which makes it inherently varied. In essence, prevailing westerly winds bring rainfall to the Atlantic coasts, which is good for plant growth, and the Gulf Stream in the Atlantic also warms coastal waters. There is no equivalent to either in the eastern part of Europe, which means it suffers from colder and drier weather.

WHAT IS EUROPE?

What 'Europe' itself means in historical terms is unclear. For a long time, the term 'Europe' was not a favoured one, as there was no consciousness of Europe as a separate space. Before the Roman Empire (initially under republican control before becoming an empire under emperors) developed in the 3rd century BCE and remained dominant in Western Europe until the early 5th century, there was scant knowledge of the geographical span of what is now Europe. Further, under Rome, this knowledge scarcely even covered Scandinavia or what is now European Russia. During this period the Mediterranean was the political and economic powerhouse, but key aspects of the Mediterranean world and the Roman Empire were outside what is now Europe, notably Egypt, Syria and Anatolia (Turkey east of the Aegean).

For long after the Roman Empire ended in Western Europe in the 5th century, Europe was not defined in terms of the empire or its continuation in the shape of the Eastern Roman Empire (Byzantium), but by many Europeans in terms of 'Christendom', the area under Christian control. Although it was politically fragmented, Christendom produced a common ideology that was more potent than anything modern Europe possesses. In addition, the medieval Papacy was a distinctive form of government for part of Christendom.

However, for Christendom it was belief and not place that counted and as a result there was no clear and permanent boundary. In fact, the Crusades that began in the 1090s very much involved an expansion of Christendom. Some of this took place within what are now parts of Europe, notably in Spain, Portugal, and on the southern and eastern shores of the Baltic, but the key area for activity was in the Near East – Israel, Palestine, Lebanon and Syria – with North Africa as a secondary sphere in the 13th century and more so from 1415, when Portuguese forces captured Ceuta in Morocco. More gains were made in Morocco and Algeria over the following 120 years.

The idea of Christendom as the definition of Europe was also problematic because of the fraught relationship between the part under the Papacy and other parts, notably that under the Eastern Roman Empire, or Byzantium. Based at Constantinople (from 1924 Istanbul), the Byzantine Empire stretched to include areas not today seen as part of Europe, such as Egypt, Syria, Israel, Lebanon and Palestine (until the 7th century) and sections of modern Turkey (into the 15th century). The modern Orthodox Church does not set a limit at what we would today geographically regard as Europe, and Orthodox views of both Europe and Christendom are very different to those of the Papacy. In particular, to the Orthodox Church, with its Patriarch based in Istanbul and obliged to be a Turkish citizen, there is no reason to leave Turkey out of Europe.

Most of the Byzantine Empire was eventually conquered by Islam and, as a result, for much of the last 600 years a large part of Eastern Europe has been part of a very different cultural and political world, that of the Ottoman Empire (Turkey). This was an Islamic imperial state, with its capital at Constantinople. Now one of Europe's most populous states, Turkey spent much of the last 600 years in conflict with Christian powers.

Discussions on admitting Turkey to the European Union underlined the problems posed by Turkish history. This is part of the wider discussion of how to consider the relationship between Europe and Islam. Such issues are dramatically illustrated by standing in Istanbul on the European side and seeing the sheer proximity of the Asian shore, or how close Tunisia is to Sicily and Malta.

To Christian contemporaries the Ottoman Empire was not so much non-European as anti-European. It defined that which was not European, both tyranny and Islam, and presented both as a threat to Christendom. The advance of Ottoman forces led to the fall of Belgrade in 1521 and Budapest in 1526, while in 1529 and 1683 the Ottomans besieged Vienna and, in 1565, Valletta in Malta. Although the later three attempts were unsuccessful, the threat they posed was very clear and remained obvious until the early 18th century when, indeed, the Ottomans took Belgrade for a second time in 1739.

Therefore, much of modern Europe was actually part of the Ottoman world, not Christendom. On the other hand, (Christian) European trans-oceanic expansion meant that from the late 15th century European influence spread across the oceans. As a result, by 1750 London, Paris and Madrid had more in common with colonial centres such as Philadelphia, Quebec and Havana, than they did with cities under Ottoman rule, such as Athens, Belgrade, Bucharest and Sofia. This situation remained the case over the following century and, albeit with a different geography and in a contrasting context, it was to resume during the Cold War with Western Europe having more in common with North America than with Eastern Europe, which, itself, looked to the Soviet Union.

This situation poses a challenge to the idea of a distinctive European history. Moreover, even if the idea is to be pressed, it is unclear how this is to be defined and, linked to this, where it is to extend. In reality, the idea that Europe has a clear set of values is fanciful, given the range of ideologies and practices that have been potent in its history.

Even so, much cultural and political capital has been invested in this approach to European history, albeit in very different ways, by the medieval Papacy, the 18th-century Enlightenment, would-be modern imperial rulers such as Napoleon and Hitler, and the European Union. For example, in 2007 Germany used its presidency of the European Union to ensure the passage of race hate laws for the entire union. But its attempt to produce a specific ban on Holocaust denial failed, not least because several member states wished to include a crime of denying, condemning, or trivializing atrocities committed in the name of Stalin, which was rejected by some other members. This illustrates the extent to which there is no common identity or history.

The Issue of Russia

Russia's role in modern European politics underlines the question of how best to approach European history. For some, Russia is presented as anti-European, as well as being a state that spans both Europe and Asia, and therefore should not be included in a history of Europe. This approach clashes with the idea of Europe as stretching eastward to the Ural mountains, and therefore including European Russia but not Asian Russia. The end of the Cold War in 1989–91 and the collapse of the Communist bloc and the Soviet Union pushed the definition of 'Europe' to the forefront as a subject of practical politics. Bound up in this issue was the question of whether

> *Ukraine and the Caucasus republics of Armenia, Azerbaijan and Georgia would be permitted to join NATO and the European Union.*

WHICH EUROPE?

Many histories of Europe focus on the Mediterranean until the end of the Roman Empire and then on France, Germany, the Low Countries (Netherlands and Belgium), and northern Italy until about 1550, after which Italy largely drops out. Scandinavia, Iberia, the Balkans, Eastern Europe, and southern Italy receive relatively little attention unless they interact with the core region of attention. Britain tends to be treated as a special case, not least by most of the British; with a tendency to regard it as a hybrid of European and non-European.

Eastern Europe has been less well covered. This reflects longstanding lower prosperity there, and its consequences for intellectual activity, as well as wartime destruction and disruption of records, notably those of landowning families, and the consequences of the Communist years (1945–89) which discouraged empirical research.

WHAT DOES 'EUROPE' MEAN TODAY?

The problem with the standard focus on Western Europe is not only that much of the continent finds its history underplayed, but also that there is an assumption that there is an inherently 'European' approach. This is misleading. Europe means different things in Madrid, Manchester, Marburg, Milan and Munich. As a result, it is necessary in reading what happens to be alive to the various accounts that can be offered – which, of course, helps make the whole idea of a 'European' history itself more interesting. The tension between would-be unity and potent difference and divergence has been a continuing theme in European history, although its particular manifestations have varied greatly. That point interacts with how we should cover European history. In particular, there is the question of the relationship between the coverage of Eastern

Europe and that of Western Europe which tends to dominate coverage of the continent as a whole.

It is worth stressing the separate feeling of local societies, within a wider whole, such that people thought of themselves as belonging to Normandy as well as France; or to Sicily and Catalonia, rather than to Italy and Spain respectively. The tension between the unity of Europe and the drive for greater autonomy among smaller groups such as Catalans and Scots leads to the question of how the map of Europe of 2050 will look compared to the Europe of 1900 or 2019. It is possible that regionalism will come to the fore. At any event, the history we will tell shows the extent to which there has been no consistent development for Europe. Instead, the powerful role of contingencies repeatedly emerge, none of which were more influential than success in war.

CHAPTER 1
THE ORIGINS OF
EUROPEAN CIVILIZATION

Beginnings to 500 BCE

Europe is a relatively new continent, one shaped by developments over the last 20,000 years. Before that, it has a long geological history shown by strata beginning with the Pre-Cambrian period, which began some 4.6 billion years ago. At various periods, there was land or sea cover, very different temperatures and vegetation, and more or less geological activity in the shape of volcanoes. Across geological time Europe was very much affected by the continental drift of tectonic plates that had occurred ever since the crust of the Earth cooled.

Europe was part of Laurasia, an enormous continent that also included North America. About 300 million years ago, this joined with Gondwanaland, the great southern continent, to form Pangaea, a supercontinent. Around 200 million to 180 million years ago Laurasia and Gondwanaland split and, later, each divided further. As a result, Eurasia (the combined landmass of Europe and Asia) separated from North Africa and was left with only a tenuous link with Africa. Subsequently, Eurasia itself was shaped within essentially its current position. Geographically, Eurasia is a key element as, from that perspective, Europe is an extension of Asia.

Human history in Europe, or at least that of organized human life, was set within a much shorter timescale of climate change, most prominently the impact of the Ice Ages and of their end at about 10,000 BCE (the last one had peaked around 18,000 BCE). On a lesser scale, subsequent global climatic changes have also been significant, such as the 'Little Ice Age' of the 14th to 17th centuries. That pattern of change remains the case today, with global warming and its particular impact on sea levels. Change is both significant and unpredictable.

PREHISTORIC HUMANS

Our understanding of human migration to Europe is rapidly changing, as new archaeological finds and the extensive use of genetics are presenting a picture of the first humans in the continent arriving earlier than had been hitherto understood. Analysis of the tooth of a 7.2 million-year-old primate *Graecopithecus* found in Greece in 2017 suggested that the skeleton shared its ancestry with the genus *Homo* and was a potential human ancestor. Footprints discovered in Crete in 2010 were left 5.7 million years ago, suggest that a bipedal hominid creature had made them.

Very different shorelines existed in this period and many Mediterranean islands were joined to the mainland, so the distinction between Africa and Europe is not as it is at present, nor are environmental considerations like rainfall levels.

Although it is difficult to be precise, given the limited and ambiguous nature of much of the evidence, there is continuing proof of the spread of humans in search of food. Climate conditions were a factor and these suggest a move out of Africa into Europe around 190,000 to 220,000 years ago. The degree of competition and conflict between the different species of hominids is not clear. The longevity and diffusion of *Homo Sapiens* is being pushed back. There is evidence of the co-existence of Neanderthals and Cro-Magnon humans, the origins of modern *Homo Sapiens*, while in 1999 a Palaeolithic skeleton with a legacy from both was discovered near Lisbon. DNA analysis indicates there was some interbreeding, with Neanderthal DNA found in modern humans. But Neanderthals came to an end as a distinct species, although the suggested dates for when this happened vary greatly.

At around 16,000 BCE the islands of Sicily and Malta were joined to Italy, Corsica was joined to Sardinia, and much of the lower Volga delta was part of a larger Caspian Sea. The geological shaping of Europe continued into the last 10,000 years and within that period the land link between Britain and continental Europe was broken (around 6500 BCE) as a result of the rise in sea level following the melting of the ice caps at the end of the last Ice Age and the release of large amounts of water. This process, and the previous glaciation linked to successive advances of the ice, each of which was followed by a retreat, also greatly affected the more detailed surface geology of much of Europe. The melting of the ice also led to the upward movement of strata that had been weighed down by the ice cap. This process is visible in the raised shorelines of coastal regions such as north-west Scotland.

Large rivers fed by snow melt gouged huge valleys, while glaciers both along their course and at their end left massive deposits of rock and sediment known as moraines. What is now the Baltic Sea was occupied 9,000 years ago by a large area of water called Lake Ancylus, which had no link to the Atlantic Ocean, while the Black Sea was not joined to the Mediterranean until about 2500 BCE. The modern regions of Europe emerged as climate and physical geography combined to produce very different outcomes, from the flat, tundra-like and cold lands of northern Europe to the hot, high mountains of southern Spain.

The end of the last Ice Age was followed by the northward movement of forest and wildlife zones, and hunter-gatherers followed. Woodlands provided shelter for animals including deer, which in turn attracted hunters. Human adaptation to the environment rapidly became the moulding of that environment, notably at the micro-level, to suit the need for habitation, foraging for and growing food, and hunting and later keeping animals. A key drive in history, this moulding was powered by the need for resources and space, and was shaped by, and, in turn, shaped, ideologies and the understanding of the environment.

In time the human species spread to much of Europe, including less hospitable areas such as the North Atlantic (where the first settlement was made on the Faroe Islands in about 825), Iceland in 874, and in Madeira probably in the early 1420s (although there are suggestions of earlier settlement there).

Early Europeans learned to find food sources, to kill, use and/or control animals, and to create shelters from what was available. For example, animal skins were used for clothing and also for settlement, with wooden poles covered by skins providing portable tents. Large animal bones, notably those of mammoths, were used in Ukraine to provide structure for shelters.

Humans also tried to establish systems of belief that would help to locate them in time and space and to make sense of their world and experiences. People retained useful objects for future use, used ideas of symmetry in their crafts, and performed tasks entailing division of labour. Although the evidence for this period is limited and affected by weathering, ploughing and other activity, there are archaeological records, such as the well-known cave paintings in Lascaux, France, and in Spain and elsewhere. For example, in Portugal cave paintings from around 15,000 BCE survive in the *Gruta do Escoural* (Escoural Cave) in the Côa Valley. Other important evidence of early human artistic life include the stylized female figurines found across Europe dating from about 23,000 BCE. These may have been linked to fertility rituals.

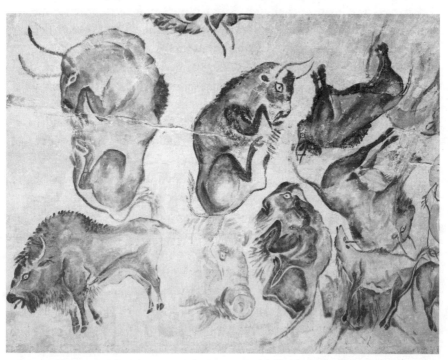

 The impressive cave paintings of bison at Altamira in Spain are an example of early human artistic endeavours.

THE BIRTH OF AGRICULTURE

The movement from merely harvesting, grinding and storing wild grains for food, to developing their cultivation, was a slow one. Farming had begun in the Middle East by around 10,000 BCE, but did not spread into Europe for another 3,000 years. Widespread use of agriculture in the continent was first seen in Greece in approximately 7000 BCE, when the first farming villages appeared. By 6000 BCE it had spread north into the Balkans and west across the Adriatic into southern Italy. By around 5000 BCE there was farming across much of Europe south of the Baltic Sea and North Sea, and later it developed in these regions too. At the same time hunting, fishing (including collecting of shellfish), and gathering wild plants continued.

The increasing yields from agriculture and the development of tools such as the plough encouraged the clearing of forests. Once they became established, agricultural skills diffused, although the pace was sometimes slow and in Europe there was no equivalent to the intensive, irrigated agriculture seen in Egypt, Iraq and China. Europe lacked the organizational structures to provide such systems, partly because its governance was simpler and its population smaller. Nonetheless, ritual centres like the vast and complex tombs of the Boyne Valley in Ireland must have taken hundreds of thousands of man-hours to construct. The spread of domestic animals – cattle, pigs, sheep and goats, brought milk, wool and an ability to pull ploughs, and was followed by wheeled vehicles.

Surviving evidence of year-round human presence increased as settlements became fixed; for example, on hilltops in the lower Tagus Valley in Portugal in about 5000 BCE. Increasingly, these settlements were not simply habitations. Instead, there was greater sophistication, for example seen in the 'causewayed' camps, ritual monuments and burial chambers in Europe from the Neolithic period (c.4000–2000 BCE). Burial centres were an important aspect of society and relationships between generations and ancestor-observance, or even worship, seems to have been important across Europe.

Although the creation of settlements was a key development, it does not cover the full range of change relating to the birth of agriculture. For example, on the Eurasian steppe in what is now European Russia, there was a more mobile culture linked to seasonal migration in search of pasture.

Megalithic Remains in Portugal
Dolmens are single-chamber megalithic (stone) tombs that can still be seen across much of Europe. The largest of these is the Anta Grande do Zambujeiro *(the Great Dolmen of Zambujeiro) near Evora in Portugal (close to the* Cromeleque dos Almendres, *a far-flung oval of 95 granite monoliths). It is thought to have been constructed around 4000–3000* BCE. *There are also megalithic burial chambers in the region around Lisbon. Stone remains provide good archaeological evidence, unlike structures built of wood or mud. Such tombs were the product of societies which have left far less evidence for their wider activities.*

METALWORKING

Between 7000 BCE and 5000 BCE people in south-east Europe and western Asia discovered an important by-product of the use of fire; namely, that heat could also be used to isolate metals from ore-bearing deposits. Soft metals, which melt at low temperatures, were the first to be used, which explains why copper was the basis of metal technology before iron. The long-lasting Stone Age began to be replaced by the successive ages of metal. Metals offered greater potency than stone, not least because they provided stronger penetration and weight, the key requirements for success in hand-to-hand combat. They were also less bulky, adding to ease of use and mobility, which was more significant because people then moved and fought on foot.

However, there were no revolutionary changes. Instead, there was a considerable overlap of flint tools (including weapons mounted in wood or bone hafts) with copper, copper with bronze, and bronze with iron, rather than a sudden and complete supplanting of one technology by another. 'Otzi', a corpse from roughly 3000 BCE found frozen in the ice of the European Alps, had a copper axe, a flint knife and flint-tipped arrows with a bow. He was wounded, if not killed, by similar weapons.

Metal weapons were generally found in more complex societies. This was especially the case once metalworking began to require the gathering of different resources, and therefore trade and the ability to finance it. Trade had developed as the flint needed for agricultural tools and axes was mined and exchanged. Salt and amber were other important goods traded over long distances. Commerce was particularly important along coasts, rivers, and hill routes above readily flooded lowlands. Individual burials with rich grave-goods (some brought by trade), suggesting a more stratified system, were a sign of these more complex societies.

The Rise of Fortifications

Archaeological research continues to provide fresh evidence of the nature of society and of the range of activity during the Bronze Age. For example, in 2012–13 sophisticated Bronze Age fortifications were discovered at La Bastida in south-eastern Spain. These included masonry walls partly flanking an entrance passage and five solid square protruding towers resting on carefully prepared foundations to prevent sliding down the steep hill, a considerable feat. There was also a water cistern. The Iron Age saw an increase in the number of hill forts, many of which were probably places of refuge as well as defensive sites where food could be stored. Hilltops were also within visual contact of each other, allowing people to send messages.

The Copper Age (*c.*4500–2200 BCE) was followed by the Bronze Age (*c.*2200–800 BCE). As a harder alloy of copper that was more effective for tools and weapons because it could hold its shape under greater pressure, bronze replaced not only copper but also hard stone and flint, which were more difficult to shape. Bronze required copper, which often had to be exported, for example from Sardinia to Greece, as well as tin. The quest for tin led to interest from Mediterranean peoples in Atlantic Europe, including in Spain, Portugal and western France, and up to Britain. The Phoenicians developed a trading base at Gadir (Cadiz) in about 800 BCE and, from there, bases in Portugal including Abul, Alcácer, Tavira and Castro Marim. The Greeks followed them. Both brought Mediterranean goods with them, including wine and textiles. Trade also became the means for technological and cultural exchange.

There was a wide-ranging process of development. The smelting of bronze was a more complex operation than using flint. Aside from trade, agriculture increased in response to the rising population, and land boundaries and, later, fields, were laid out, notably from the second millennium BCE.

After the Bronze Age, the smelting and forging of iron spread from western Asia into Europe during the Iron Age. The dating for this varies depending on the part of Europe under consideration. In the Aegean it began in about 1190 BCE, but in Northern Europe not till about 500 BCE. The production of iron developed in central Europe by about 1000 BCE and then spread throughout Europe, reaching Britain by the 8th century BCE. The use of iron hoes and nails brought a new flexibility to agriculture and construction. Marginal areas were increasingly cleared of trees and cultivated. Iron made wagons more durable and made better weapons because it was less likely to shatter, especially when carbon was added to produce steel.

THE BIRTH OF WRITING

The representation of language through graphic means developed differently across the world, with particular contrasts between hieroglyphs (picture writing) and alphabetic writing. The writing of language followed that of numbers and was probably in existence in Sumer (Mesopotamia) and Egypt by around 3100 BCE. From there, writing spread into Europe, initially to Greece, and from there variants of the Phoenician alphabet were introduced to what is now mainland Italy further west. Italian numerical systems were also heavily influenced by Greece.

There is a distinction between proto-writing and true writing, and clearly the invention of writing was a gradual process, like many other inventions. Written symbols came to stand for sounds or concepts and permitted the retention and diffusion of information, so these could be used to codify regulations. The most famous writing script from the period is 'Linear B', which was used for writing Mycenaean Greek. The oldest such writing dates to about 1450 BCE and is descended from 'Linear A', an earlier and as-yet undeciphered script used for representing the Minoan language from about 2500 BCE to 1450 BCE, which was used alongside Cretan hieroglyphics dating from about 2100 BCE to 1700 BCE. Linear B ceased to exist with the fall of Mycenaean civilization and evidence of writing stopped, until the Greeks adopted and adapted the Phoenician alphabet.

MYCENAE AND MINOA

Two societies led the way in Bronze Age Europe – Minoan Crete and Mycenaean Greece. While merchants took wares from Italy to Greece to transalpine Europe and Spain, it was along the shores of the Mediterranean that the most notable societies developed.

Minoan Crete was a palace-based society that emerged in the island of Crete around 2000 BCE, taking its name from the legendary king, Minos. The civilization was suddenly extinguished in 1450 BCE by a volcanic explosion. Today, the extensive ruins of the palace of Knossos, with its complex architecture and detailed wall paintings, hint at the sophistication of the society that created it.

The city of Mycenae, strategically located on the road between the two major ports of Argos and Corinth, had established itself as the major power in the Greek peninsula by around 1550 BCE. The city itself served as both palace and fortress and at its height housed as many as 30,000 people. New settlements grew up across Greece and elaborate burials for its leaders represented just some of the wealth that was generated. Buoyed by trade, raiding and agriculture, Mycenaean Greece developed a written language, a complex economy and new styles of art that formed an important precursor to the classical societies that followed it.

Mycenaean society was very much that of a warrior élite presiding over peasantry, a situation seen more generally across Europe. There were also slaves, as in other parts of Europe, but their status is unclear. In the Linear B documents of Minoan Crete from about 1600 BCE, *doeros* and *doera*

 A fresco of a woman from the Acropolis of Mycenae, 13th century BCE, hints at the refinement of Mycenaean society.

were mentioned at Knossos in Crete and the Mycenaean site of Pylos in the Peloponnese, but it is unclear whether these terms meant male and female slaves. Some were referred to as the property of living individuals, but others, especially at Pylos, were described as belonging to a god or goddess and had a status different to that of other slaves, as they could have leases on land and seem to have lived like ordinary free persons.

Interactions with the wider world tended to be south- and east-facing, looking to developed civilizations of the Levant, Mesopotamia and North Africa. Archaeological findings have shown evidence of contact with the Assyrians, Egyptians, Phoenicians and Mittani. Trade with southern Italy was also common. However, Crete's interaction with the Hittites of Anatolia, a landward society, appears to have been more limited.

Gods and Monsters
Mycenaean Greece attained its fame partly through the writings of Homer, who used its history, and particularly the legendary story of

the siege of Troy, as the basis of his great epic The Iliad. *Featuring capricious gods and mythical creatures such as harpies, the Sphinx and the one-eyed giant Polyphemus, Homer, in both the* The Iliad *and* The Odyssey, *presented humans as just one of many forces competing for power in the world.*

Mycenaean civilization came to an end in around 1100 BCE, possibly following invasion by the 'Sea Peoples'. This is an obscure period and process and the identity and origins of the invaders are particularly unclear. A more widespread collapse of civilizations in the eastern Mediterranean was underway in the 12th century BCE. Powerful cultures like the Hittite empire (in modern-day Turkey) and the leading cities of Syria and Canaan collapsed. The crises were triggered by a combination of invasion, internal rebellion and possible environmental catastrophes, including volcanic eruptions, leading to widespread disruption of international trade and state hierarchies.

The end of the Bronze Age came with violent convulsions. The period that followed has been described as the Greek Dark Ages. It would not be until more than 500 years later that another civilization would emerge in Europe that could match the power and prestige of the Mycenaeans. This matching was provided by the revival of Greek culture.

CHAPTER 2
THE CLASSICAL WORLD

*c.*500 BCE–500 CE

The Classical world's legacy of history for modern Europe is more obvious than that left by earlier periods. Not all of the Classical world left a lasting influence; it was Greece and Rome that really did so. Early on they were minor forces compared to the empires of Egypt and the Middle East. But the Greeks, and even more so the Romans, successively became forces in the development of Western civilization. This civilization was to look to Greece and Rome, rather than to Mesopotamia or Egypt, which is important to the lineage and identity of European culture.

PERSIAN AGGRESSION AND ANCIENT GREECE

The link between Mycenaean Greece and what came later is unclear. There was a 'Dark Ages' from about 1100 BCE until the 8th century BCE. Archaeological evidence for this period is limited, but the resumption of writing in the 8th century BCE was linked to the rise of city states, particularly in the Greek world, but also with the Etruscans in northern and central Italy.

City states were individual cities that dominated their hinterlands, and they varied in importance. Sparta and Corinth were key players in Greece and from the 480s BCE so was Athens, which used its substantial silver mines as the basis to build a large fleet. Trade was essential to city-state life, especially within the locality that generated their food, but also longer range. Citizen militias were the military arm of these city states. Citizen 'hoplite' soldiers (infantry fighting in phalanx formations in pitched battles and providing disciplined force) helped to settle disputes between city states speedily, so that agricultural life could be resumed.

The wide-ranging Persian empire created in the 6th century BCE built up a formidable navy, which it deployed to become a major force in

 The city-state of Corinth was one of the wealthiest and most powerful actors in the ancient Greek world.

the Aegean. Having conquered the Greek cities in Ionia on the eastern shores of the Aegean in 546–45 BCE, the Persians responded to a rebellion there in 499 BCE by crushing it in 494 BCE and then turning against Greece itself. At this point the Persians were already a major force in the Balkans. Darius I (r.522–486 BCE), an active expansionist, had invaded Thrace in 513 BCE and conquered the lands south of the River Danube on and near the coast of what is now Bulgaria. Moving across the Danube, he found the Scythians a far more difficult challenge because they used a classic technique of nomadic warfare, avoiding conflict and, instead, destroying both food and wells. Darius retreated, then pressed on south-westwards, capturing Greek cities on the northern shores of the Aegean and making the kingdom of Macedon (Macedonia) a vassal state.

In response to the Ionian rising, Darius decided to punish Athens and Eretria (on the island of Euboea), which had provided support. In 490 BCE an amphibious force destroyed Eretria, before landing at Marathon on Attica (the region including Athens). A rapid Athenian response, however, led to the defeat of this force. The Battle of Marathon became crucial to the Athenian sense of their special destiny.

In 480 BCE a mighty Persian army under its king Xerxes crossed the Hellespont (Dardanelles) on a bridge of boats and moved south into Greece. This campaign was to be crucial to the destiny of Europe. The Persian conquest of Egypt in 525 BCE led by Cambyses II had already showed that there was no necessary limit to the extent of its empire. Along with the conquest of Ionia, it also demonstrated that the geographical concept of continents did not determine political bodies and their boundaries. This was demonstrated even more clearly in 480 BCE, when many Greek states remained neutral (and Thessaly and Boeotia both allied with Xerxes). Athens then became the key source of resistance north of the Peloponnese. An attempt to hold the pass at Thermopylae against the advancing Persians was outflanked by the Persians and the Greeks withdrew, leaving a small, largely Spartan, rearguard that famously fought to the death.

The Persians captured Athens but at Salamis in 480 BCE their navy was defeated, with the Athenians using a particularly effective war galley called a trireme. After Salamis, Xerxes and part of his army returned to Asia, but his son-in-law Mardonius was left with the rest of the army. At Plataea in 479 BCE the Persian army was defeated by an alliance of Greek city states including Athens, Corinth and Sparta, and the Persian fleet was also defeated by the Greeks at Cape Mycale. As a result, the Persians lost control of the areas of Greece they had conquered the previous year. The Persians then retreated to Asia Minor and the Greeks drove them from Thrace, the Hellespont and Ionia.

After these conflicts the powerful cities of Sparta and Athens formed leagues of cities. Athens led the Delian League, established in 478 BCE with its treasury on the island of Delos. Even so, Sparta and Athens were unable to convert these leagues into durable empires, and competition between the two alliance systems led to the Peloponnesian War (431–404 BCE). For many years, neither side was able to prevail, as Sparta was superior on land but Athens dominated at sea. Spartan armies advanced on Athens, but the Athenians took shelter behind their city walls. However, in 415 BCE Athens unwisely sent an expedition to Syracuse in Sicily, and its total defeat in 413 BCE was eventually followed by the surrender of Athens. Thucydides' *History of the Peloponnesian War*, recounting this conflict, was one of the first major historical works.

499–479 BCE	*Persian Wars*
499 BCE	*Ionian Revolt*
490 BCE	*Battle of Marathon*
480 BCE	*Battle of Thermopylae*
480 BCE	*Battle of Salamis*
479 BCE	*The Persian Army is defeated at Plataea*
431–404 BCE	*Peloponnesian War*
415–413 BCE	*Athenian expedition to Sicily*
371 BCE	*Thebes defeats Sparta in the Battle of Leuctra*
359–336 BCE	*Reign of Philip II of Macedon*
357 BCE	*Macedon defeats the Illyrians*
353–2 BCE	*Macedonian invasion of Thessaly*
337 BCE	*Creation of the League of Corinth*
336 BCE	*Assassination of Philip II and the coronation of Alexander the Great*
333 BCE	*Battle of Issus*
331 BCE	*Battle of Gaugamela*
323 BCE	*Death of Alexander the Great*

The defeat of Athens was followed by continued disunity in Greece. Sparta was the major power, until it was defeated by the forces of the city state of Thebes at Leuctra in 371 BCE. In 338 BCE the autonomy of the divided Greek city states fell victim to the new imperial power of Macedon, following defeat at Chaeronea. Macedon, to the north of Greece, was a part of the Greek world that, like the kingdom of Epirus to the north-west, was regarded as somewhat barbarian by many Greeks. Unlike Classical Greece, Macedon was a kingdom, not a number of city states. Philip II of Macedon (r.359–336 BCE) was the key figure in the rise of Macedon. His military skill was crucial and he focused on remodelling the army, notably by introducing the 'Sarissa', or very long spear, which was used by the phalanx of infantry. Lengthy conflict led to Philip's defeat of the Illyrians (357 BCE) and of Athenian attempts to control the coastline of northern Greece (359–354 BCE). Invading Thessaly in 353–352 BCE, Philip balanced his efforts between intervention further south in Greece and further north and west, notably against the Thracians into modern Bulgaria (342 BCE). After the victory at Chaeronea on 2 August 338 BCE Philip created and led the League of Corinth, a Greek league. This was designed as the basis for the invasion of Persia that was actually carried out by Philip's son, Alexander.

Meanwhile, Greece had developed important models of political organization, with different governmental systems. These were based, like Greek culture as a whole, on city life. The *polis*, or self-governing city, was the key unit. The renowned Greek philosopher Aristotle (384–322 BCE) argued that the pursuit of public culture and virtue was possible in city states. As an expression of their identity, Greek cities constructed impressive public buildings such as the Parthenon in Athens, building of which started in 448 BCE.

 The city of Athens spent much of the 5th century BCE in competition with the rival city of Sparta.

Many cities were under dictators, who were referred to as tyrants. Sparta, a heavily militaristic society, had kings, but their power was limited. Other cities, notably Athens, relied on democracy, in the shape of votes by adult male freemen, and this was also to be the model in Republican Rome. Although there was a relatively large electorate, women lacked the vote and so did slaves. Rural areas were under the control of cities and rural life was regarded as less civilized. The differences between the city states and their disunity matched the Greek depiction of their quarrelsome gods.

The variety and complexity of Greek culture are readily illustrated by counterpointing slavery and the theatre, which is linked to the playwrights Aeschylus, Euripides and Sophocles. Characterization was developed by these writers, who displayed a marked ability to innovate and to move beyond a religious identity for drama. Other significant cultural developments included architecture and sculpture, both of which were to have a farflung influence and to have a key constitutive element in the Western self-image. Greek architecture saw a focus on religion, with building in stone leaving major temples such as those of the Parthenon in Athens and the Temple of Concordia in Agrigento, Sicily. Sculpture in marble produced effective representations of the human figure.

Magna Graecia

Greek settlers were not restricted to modern Greece and the Aegean coast of modern Turkey. The independent city states of Magna Graecia (Greater Greece) were established along the coasts of Sicily (from 734 BCE) and southern Italy. These settlers were possibly affected by overpopulation in Greece and/or were seeking new opportunities, a process later to be seen very differently with the Vikings. The city states spread Greek culture westwards and reflected the significance of maritime commercial links. The ruins of several of the cities, notably Agrigento, Segesta, Selinus and Syracuse in Sicily, and of Paestum, Metaponto and Policoro in southern Italy, remain most impressive. Compared to these settlements Rome must have seemed rather primitive. Nevertheless, Rome had conquered southern Italy by 250 BCE and went on to conquer Greece and also the Greek city state of Massilia (Marseilles), which had been founded in about 600 BCE. As a result, Greek commercial networks became part of the Roman world.

Greek influence expanded with the establishment of colonies from the 9th century BCE onwards. This reflected its maritime links and was seen around the Black Sea from the 7th century BCE and into the western Mediterranean from the 9th century BCE. Byzantium (Istanbul today) was founded in about 660 BCE and was one of a number of colonies that guarded the route from the Black Sea into the Aegean. There was no comparable pattern of colonization into the interior, for example along river routes such as the Rhône, Danube and Dnieper, in contrast to later Viking colonization and settlement activity along the Russian rivers.

The Greeks traded goods such as their metalwork from their coastal colonies and did reach the peoples of the interior, like the Scythians of southern Russia. The path of these goods can be charted in grave remains, notably those of Celts from the 6th century as well as in Scythian graves. In return, the Greeks obtained raw materials such as food and amber, with Athens becoming reliant on grain from the Black Sea.

THE INFLUENCE OF ALEXANDER THE GREAT

In 356 BCE the man who would be known as Alexander the Great was born. His father, Philip II of Macedon, had unified the Greek city states and created a formidable force in the Mediterranean. After Philip's assassination in 336 BCE Alexander took the throne, determined to expand on his father's achievements. The greatest threat still facing the Greeks was the Persian empire. Seeking to establish security, Alexander invaded Asia Minor (modern Turkey) in 334 BCE, where he won a battle against a larger force at Issus (333 BCE). Following his success, he turned south to conquer Syria and Egypt, before heading east, crushing Darius at Gaugamela (331 BCE) in modern Iraq and then advancing via modern Iran and Afghanistan into the Indian subcontinent. He died in Babylon in 323 BCE, aged just 32.

Alexander was succeeded by a series of warring generals in the Hellenistic period. Struggles from 321 BCE produced rival kingdoms including Macedon (ruled by the Antigonids from 306 BCE to 168 BCE), Egypt (ruled by the Ptolemies), and Syria, Iraq, Persia and southern Turkey (ruled by the Seleucids).

As a result of Alexander's overthrow of the Persian empire there was no longer a threat to Greece from the east. Instead, Greek culture spread into large parts of Asia as well as Egypt. At this point, it was not helpful to think of 'Europe' or its limits.

Macedon's dominance of Greece was soon challenged by independent Greek states, some of which created leagues such as the Aetolian League and the Achaean League, which captured Corinth in 243 BCE. Athens and Sparta were also among the independent states, but Macedon remained the key power. Greek disunity provided an opportunity for Roman intervention and later, in 148–146 BCE, for Roman conquest. This conquest was demonstrated most clearly in the brutal sack of captured Corinth in 146 BCE.

A mosaic depicting Alexander the Great (left) fighting Darius I at the Battle of Issus in 333 BCE.

THE ETRUSCANS

Before Rome rose to prominence in the Italian peninsula, the Etruscans were the most powerful regional force. The Etruscans lived in effectively a confederation of city states based in present-day Tuscany in northern central Italy, an area then known as Etruria. They became dominant in central Italy by the 7th century and their power peaked in about 530 BCE, when they expanded into the Po Valley. The Etruscans also established themselves in Campania, around Naples. As well as their agriculture, the Etruscans drew on copper and iron mines and initially the Romans relied heavily on the Etruscans' impressive ability to cast iron, construct arches and produce portraits. Their tombs and the tomb paintings remain impressive, but a lack of literary records leaves them obscure. This is true of much early European history.

In 524 BCE the Etruscans were repulsed from Cumae, a Greek city near Naples. However, it was Rome that was to be their fatal enemy. In

 The Tomb of the Leopards from c.450 BCE was part of the large Etruscan Monterozzi necropolis to the east of Tarquinia in Italy.

396 BCE, Veii, one of the Etruscan League of 12 cities, was conquered by Rome. Southern Etruria was conquered by the Romans by 350 BCE, and all of Etruria by 260 BCE. Etruscan language and culture subsequently collapsed and were absorbed by those of Rome.

THE EARLY HISTORY OF ROME

Supposedly founded in 753 BCE by twin brothers Romulus and Remus, who had been rescued from abandonment and suckled by a she-wolf, the account of Rome's origins is a useful legend rather than accurate history. In fact, Rome was probably a village for at least a century earlier. Rome was ruled by kings until Tarquin, apparently a brutal oppressor, was driven out by nobles who created a republic in 509 BCE. Wars for survival eventually became wars for expansion.

At the same time, the Romans proved adept at cementing their expansion by granting citizenship, gaining allies and establishing colonies of Roman citizens. Having become the most powerful of the Italian, or Latin, city states as a result of a series of conflicts ending in 338 BCE, the Romans pressed on to defeat other peoples in central Italy, notably the Samnites, who were finally defeated in 290 BCE after wars in 343–341 BCE, 326–304 BCE, and 298–290 BCE. Gains in these wars were consolidated by establishing colonies of Latin citizens.

Rome eventually unified the Italian peninsula through lengthy and inexorable campaigning. This included resistance to Celtic attacks from the north and to invasion in 280 BCE by Pyrrhus, king of Epirus in Greece, on behalf of the Greek settlements in Italy. Pyrrhus was an effective general whose army included elephants. Initially successful, he was finally defeated by Rome in 275 BCE, which led to his return to Epirus. His reign (307–272 BCE) again demonstrated the extent to which the sea, in this case the Adriatic, was seen as a medium of power and activity rather than a barrier to expansion. The Celts of northern Italy were defeated by the Romans in 224–222 BCE and rebellions were then crushed. The Romans pressed on into southern Gaul (France) in 125–121 BCE. As with the sea, mountain ranges, in this case the Alps, were not seen as limits. Rome was Italy's Sparta: bellicose and picking its leaders accordingly. Julius Caesar was to be the product of this society.

THE PUNIC WARS

Rome became a great power as a result of successive victories in the three Punic Wars over Carthage, an empire based on the city of Carthage near modern Tunis that ruled Sardinia, Sicily, parts of southern and eastern Spain and much of modern Tunisia. The range of the Carthaginian Empire shows the extent to which at this time Europe was not a unit, and certainly not one defined by geography. The same is shown by Greek settlements in Ionia (the Aegean coast of Turkey) and with Roman expansion. Instead, boundaries were to emerge eventually, and only as a result of war and settlement.

The First Punic War (264–241 BCE) focused on the control of Sicily, which, like most of the rest of Europe, was a geographical rather than a political unit. The Romans won after a bitter conflict in which they had to learn how to operate as an effective naval power, winning a major battle off Economus in 256 BCE. Sicily was to be a major source of grain for Rome. (Reliable grain sources were crucial to stability and power, as well as expressions of strength.) After this war Rome also acquired control of Sardinia. As a result, the First Punic War left Rome even more clearly dominant in mainland Italy.

The Second Punic War (218–201 BCE) is famous for the march of the leading Carthaginian general Hannibal (247–183 BCE) from Spain across southern France and the Alps and his invasion of Italy. Although he was brilliantly successful (notably at Cannae in 216 BCE, where his forces inflicted about 50,000 Roman casualties) Hannibal could not knock Rome out of the war. By taking the war to North Africa, the Romans forced Carthage to surrender.

Rome's victory established its dominance in the western Mediterranean, including eastern and southern Spain, which became important sources of minerals and food for the Roman Empire. From this point onwards Rome would not face so wide-ranging an opponent, which meant it was more able to prioritize and direct resources against opponents and, as a result, to dictate the strategic pace.

THE END OF THE REPUBLIC

Having defeated Hannibal, the Romans pressed on. They had taken control of the eastern Mediterranean, Egypt, Gaul (France) and Spain by 30 CE, following up with most of Britain and the Balkans by 100 CE, notably by annexing Thrace in 45 CE. Egypt was a major source of grain for Rome. Julius Caesar was the key figure in the conquest of Gaul from 58 BCE, most dramatically by overcoming the Celtic tribal leader Vercingetorix, his major opponent, in 52 BCE by successfully besieging him in the hilltop town of Alesia. Caesar's *Gallic Wars* is a major source for Roman military history.

Yet this process, including Caesar's conquest of Gaul, was far from easy. For example, in Iberia the Romans found there was a major difference between overthrowing another foreign imperial presence, in the shape of Carthage, and subjugating the rest of Iberia. The former was more vulnerable to attack and more focused on cities, notably ports, that could be besieged and where resources could be focused for attack. But in the rest of Iberia the targets were far more diffuse and this helps to explain how long it took for the Romans to conquer Spain and Portugal, where resistance continued until 17 BCE.

Alternative commitments were also significant, notably the series of wars with Macedon (214–205 BCE, 200–197 BCE, 171–168 BCE, 150–148 BCE) that left Rome in control of Macedon and Greece, but that absorbed much of her energy through to 148 BCE. Roman victories at Cynoscephalae (197 BCE) and especially Pydna (168 BCE) were crucial, but these battles were close-run things and it is unclear that the Roman legion was superior to the phalanx. The Romanized Greek historian Polybius' claim to this effect was largely Roman propaganda aimed at discouraging further Greek revolts. The Greeks argued that the Romans had been lucky. In practice the Romans had superior manpower, resources, willpower and organization.

Meanwhile, strains within Rome led to the fall of the Republic. Major military commanders used their strength to dominate Rome, firstly Marius and Sulla in the 80s BCE, and then Pompey and Julius Caesar. The intertwining of politics and the military proved a key problem for the Republic. Ambitious politicians such as Caesar sought military command on the frontiers, then tried to have resources directed to their campaigning, like Napoleon did later with Revolutionary France in the 1790s. A civil war between Pompey, who presented himself as the champion of the Senate, and Caesar in 49–46 BCE led to the defeat and death of Pompey.

Caesar sought to change the republic. Although an aristocrat by birth and upbringing, Caesar was a leading *popularis*, a member of the political group that drew much of its support from the common people of Rome. An opposition conspiracy led to his assassination in Rome on the Ides of March (15 March) in 44 BCE and then to a civil war in which a triumvirate of Caesar's supporters eventually defeated the conspirators at Philippi in Greece in 42 BCE. The triumvirate, which included Caesar's

Julius Caesar led the conquest of Gaul in the 1st century BCE and his writings have become a key source for understanding the military history of Rome.

heir Octavian and the politician and general Mark Antony, fell out and Octavian emerged victorious in 30 BCE.

Mark Antony allied with Cleopatra, the ruler of Egypt, who became his lover. His resistance to Octavian's rule was extinguished when he was totally defeated in a great naval battle at Actium in 31 BCE. The successful Octavian assumed the title Augustus and established himself as emperor. Pressing his advantage, he seized Egypt in 30 BCE and claimed he had finally brought peace to Rome.

THE ROMAN SYSTEM

The Roman system rested on the idea of citizenship. Being a citizen was a basis for equality, but, as with Britain in the 19th century, the situation was very different for rich and poor, men and women, parents and children, eldest sons and others. For example, free tenant farmers were citizens not slaves, but were in a bad position economically and had to pay rents and taxes. They were mostly to become serfs (peasants with few rights). In contrast, major landowners and tenants-in-chief were in a far more attractive situation. In order to help bring stability and military manpower, citizenship was eventually extended to all adult male Italians in the 1st century BCE, and to all males who were not slaves in 212 CE.

The empire sent products to the city of Rome and around the empire and, within a free trade system unprecedented in Europe until recent decades, benefited from economies of scale and the diffusion of new goods and best practices. Following their conquests, the Romans established large agricultural estates and developed viticulture (wine production) and the cultivation of grain, olives and vines. They also sought to develop and expand the production of minerals and metals, such as silver and tin in Spain and Britain.

Roman civilization was based on an urban culture and forms of organization, and cities were founded across the Roman world. Many have lasted to the present, such as Cologne, Lisbon and London. Communications were a key element. Major shipping routes were anchored by impressive ports such as Lisbon, London and Ostia near Rome. Cities were also often built at the junctions of roads, for example Braga in Portugal.

The Roman aqueduct 'Pont del Diable' in Tarragona, Spain, dates back to the reign of the emperor Augustus.

Precious Metals

Recent archaeological excavations have greatly expanded our knowledge of Roman mineral production. In 2014 major gold mines from the 1st century BCE were found in Las Médulas in northwest Spain. It has been suggested that this was the largest mining gold pit in the Roman world, and was one in which hydraulic systems were used to bring high pressure water to the site for processing. In 2017 archaeologists excavating the city of Munigua in southern Spain found a large mining operation for copper and iron using ventilated underground galleries so that miners could go even deeper in pursuit of the deposits. The mines had been in use earlier, notably by the Carthaginians, but the Romans greatly increased production there.

Cities drove Romanization because they were the locations to which the wealth generated in the countryside was transferred, notably through taxes, rent and expenditure. Landowners tended to live in the cities, where Roman dress and the Latin language were adopted. Aqueducts brought water into the cities. Recent archaeological excavations continue to provide evidence of Romanization, including evidence of a large 4th century Roman palace in Córdoba, Spain. There are also sites that are still only partially excavated, for example in Portugal.

Romanization was much weaker in areas that were mountainous and/ or remote from cities, and where the economy was more a matter of subsistence and/or pastoral agriculture, for example in north-west Spain. In these areas, pre-Roman pagan practices tended to continue.

BEYOND THE ROMAN WORLD

Warrior societies dominated the world to the north of the Roman Empire. The spread of Indo-European groups migrating over a long period of time, at least as far back as 2000 BCE, greatly affected Europe. Improving archaeological knowledge means the Celtic peoples of the 1st millennium BCE have become a more distinctive group than their predecessors. They appeared in southern Germany in about 800 BCE and then spread over much of France, and from there more widely. Having crossed the Pyrenees into Spain, the Celts moved into Portugal in about 700 BCE, building fortified hill villages or *citânias* such as the Citânia de Briteiros, which was inhabited from about 300 BCE. Protected by walls and supported by a water distribution system, it contained over 150 stone huts linked by paved paths.

The Celts also pressed hard on Rome, sacking it in 390 BCE and occupying northern Italy, which the Romans called Cisalpine Gaul or 'Gaul this side of the Alps'. The Celts also attacked Macedon, defeating it in 281 BCE and invading Greece in 279 BCE, only to be defeated by Macedon at Lysimachia in Thrace in 277 BCE. This was an important event in European history but one that tends to be underplayed due to a relative neglect of Balkan history.

The extent of Celtic influence can be a controversial subject. For example, features of Celtic settlement, culture and civilization have

 Citânia de Briteiros was a Celtic settlement located in northern Portugal.

been found in southern England, but it is unclear how much was due to a widespread population movement, or more limited immigration, or trade. It is likely that all three played a role. Celtic societies had proto-towns (larger and more complex settlements), coins, and tribal 'states' with chieftain patterns of tribal organization and populations of tens of thousands, although without sophisticated governmental activity. The Celts were dominant across much of Europe but were driven from modern Romania by its inhabitants, the Dacians, in the 2nd century BCE while many Celtic tribes were subjugated by the Romans, in northern Italy, Spain, Portugal, France and England.

Trade
Trade provides a very different aspect of the world beyond Rome. The Romans traded widely within their empire, helped by a single currency, the rule of law, good communications and support for trade. They also traded beyond the empire in Europe, Africa and Asia. Within Europe, the key imports were amber from the Baltic and slaves. Into Asia, the Romans traded across the Silk Road and also from the Red Sea.

Further from Roman control, the Germanic peoples were an Indo-European ethnolinguistic group that appear to have emerged in southern Scandinavia during the Nordic Bronze Age of 1700–500 BCE, before moving south at the expense of Celts and also clashing with the Romans. This occurred most notably in 102–101 BCE, when the Cimbri and Teutones invaded southern France and northern Italy only to be defeated, and subsequently, more consistently, on the Danube and Rhine frontiers. Other Germanic tribes moved into Eastern Europe.

From the 4th century these tribes were affected by invaders from the Asian interior including the Huns, who forced westward the Ostrogoths and Visigoths, major Germanic tribes, in 376. This process is relatively obscure. It interacted with the complexity of the relationship between Rome and the Germanic tribes, as well as with the peoples living to the north of the Roman Empire who were perceived as 'barbarians' by the Romans while also being partly Romanized by their contact with them. This is demonstrated in the way that many Visigoths and other Germanic tribespeople initially formed Roman military units before turning on the Romans, in part because Rome did not know how to manage them. The search for land was a key factor, notably when the Vandals, Suevi and Alans crossed the frozen River Rhine in 406, and so was pressure from the highly mobile Huns. After overwhelming the Alans to the north of the Caucasus in about 370, the Huns pressed west under Attila (r.c.444–53) and invaded Italy and France.

AUGUSTUS AND THE EARLY EMPERORS

Augustus had no palace, court, or regalia. The machinery of the Republic continued to operate and his military command was formally limited in both space and time. His personal position and popularity were unique, but that did not make him an 'emperor' in any meaningful sense. In fact, referring to Augustus as emperor anticipates what his successors turned the system into.

He also had to compromise abroad. Much of western Germany was conquered from 12 BCE but a major defeat in the Teutoburg Forest in 9 CE led to the loss of three legions, the region's abandonment and a retreat to the Rhine frontier. In contrast, the establishment of the provinces of Moesia, Raetia, Noricum and finally Pannonia in 9 CE, marked an advance to the Danube, which remained the frontier.

Lasting stability eluded Augustus' successors. This was partly due to divisions within the ruling family and the inadequacies of his successors, especially Caligula (r.37–41 CE), who was either mad or behaved in a way that critics could present as mad. He introduced Hellenistic court practices which favoured autocracy, and was assassinated. The Praetorian Guard, or imperial bodyguard, forced the Senate to recognize Claudius (r.41–54 CE) as emperor, rather than restore the republic. Claudius invaded Britain in 43 CE to gain a military reputation and win popularity with the Roman legions.

The divisions interacted with tensions within the ruling élite, tensions that brought together ideological differences, kinship rivalries, links within and into the ruling family, and particular political issues. There was also the longstanding problem of military control. The government's desire to monopolize force and to insist on strict central control naturally conflicted with autonomous frontier units whose commanders could launch bids for power. This was very clearly shown in 68–9 CE when the unpopularity of the volatile and unstable Nero (r.54–68 CE) led to his death, and four commanders trying to seize their opportunity. The eventual victor was Vespasian (r.69–79 CE), who created the new and effective Flavian imperial dynasty (r.69–96 CE). However, this entrenched the practice of the army making and unmaking emperors. The elderly Nerva (r.96–98 CE) found his lack of military experience a problem and adopted the experienced general Trajan (r.98–117 CE) as his son and successor. Trajan was followed by his protégé Hadrian (r.117–38 CE), another experienced general. Both were Romans born in Spain, demonstrating the empire's ability to draw on and reward talent.

In 107 CE after difficult campaigning, the Romans under Trajan established Dacia, a province north of the Danube in what is now western Romania, which Rome held until 270. Similarly, in what is now south-west Germany, Rome created a province in 83 CE but abandoned it in about 260. With these exceptions, the northern border of the empire was on the Rhine, the Danube and in northern England, notably on

Hadrian's Wall, while what is now Crimea was a vassal kingdom from 63 CE. The Roman Empire reached its height in terms of stability under Marcus Aurelius (r.161–80 CE), although he had to restore the Danube frontier after an invasion by Germanic tribes.

Rome built defensive walls, notably between the upper Rhine and the upper Danube, which proved to be formidable. They were supported by fortresses and provided a limited physical barrier but also an excellent observation and early-warning system when combined with regularly spaced lookout posts. They were able to communicate rapidly, using flag or light signals. Centrally-placed reserve forces were held back and could then respond rapidly to the main incursions once they had been identified. This practice meant that Rome achieved economy of force without tying down large numbers of troops. Fortresses provided both sites for defence and bases for attack, while the walls served not only to control 'barbarians,' but also as an economic influence zone, a source of intelligence catchment, a means to impose order on local citizens, and a way to regulate trade.

THE FALL OF ROME

The pressures of attack from outside the Roman Empire and the response of new governmental divisions within it led to the centre of power moving to the new capital of Byzantium (now Istanbul), which was renamed Constantinople by Emperor Constantine I in 330. He had converted to Christianity in 312 and defeated his rival Maxentius at the battle of the Milvian Bridge in the same year. Constantine went on to become sole ruler from 324 until his death in 337.

Constantine's conversion was followed by the downgrading of paganism. This conversion, which was maintained in battle with supporters of the old ways, greatly disrupted notions of continuity. Christians had long been publicly martyred and monotheistic (one God) Christianity challenged the system of the Olympian gods, a polytheistic system that allowed the incorporation of the emperors into the religious pantheon. The divisiveness arising from this change weakened the empire when it should have been concentrating on external threats. Byzantium became the city of the new, and Rome represented the old, its social disparities making the equality propounded by Christianity seem particularly subversive.

Agriculture and Population Growth in the Roman Europe
Farming methods improved during the Roman period and this was important to the ability of Europe to support greater numbers of people, disease permitting. In the late 3rd and 4th centuries the use of larger ploughs spread and coulters were added, leading to the cutting of deeper furrows and allowing for the working of heavier soils. The introduction of two-handed scythes enabled hay to be cut faster and larger quantities to be stored for winter forage. Corn-drying kilns were constructed and crop rotation spread, while animals were overwintered in hay meadows. Animal or water-powered mills became a significant feature.

Imperial authority was also contested. This involved competition to be emperor and also regional commanders pursuing quasi-independence, sometimes in preparation for bids for imperial power. These commanders included Postumus in the 260s and Magnus Maximus in the 380s.

Economic problems were highly significant and there is clear evidence of a decline in agricultural production, industry and trade by the later 2nd century. The causes are unclear, though it seems that climate change may have been a factor.

Many of the economic concerns behind the fall of Rome were related to power politics. Rome lost resources as a result of inroads, and notably so not only in the west of the empire but also of its east, where frequent pressure was exerted by the Sassanians who took control of Persia and then pressed westward. The Romans also lost control of their trade into the Indian Ocean, where the hundreds of Roman gold coins found in southern India testify to its range. Economic problems affected imperial finances, and the weight and precious metal content in Rome's currency fell, which made it harder to win support.

In the end the Eastern Empire held off the Sassanians, just as earlier the

Parthians had been thwarted. However, pressure on the Western Empire from 'barbarians' proved more successful from the late 3rd century, and even more the late 4th century. As the frontier defences and the economy was badly hit so it became impossible to maintain the military effort.

The 'barbarian' invasions themselves were a complex process, as some of the resistance was mounted by similar peoples: Germans made up much of the Roman field army in the 4th and 5th centuries, and some invaders or would-be invaders were recruited to help against others.

There was also a major shift in Roman strategy under the pressure of increased attacks. The policy of strong frontier defence based on permanent border garrisons, which had been the norm from the late 1st century CE to about 235, as with Hadrian's Wall in northern England, was abandoned in favour of a defence in depth, relying on mobile field armies as the key element of a system using fixed fortifications. In Gaul about 100 urban centres were fortified with impressive stone walls. The ostensible purpose of these field armies, in which cavalry played a greater role than before, was to move out to meet invaders. However, their primary function often became that of the protection of the emperor from internal rivals. This emphasis ensured that provinces were left susceptible to invasion, which sapped both resources and political support.

The political role of the army was such that several emperors in the 3rd century (including Diocletian) were Illyrian soldiers from the western Balkans, a region that was a major recruiting base for the army. 'Barbarian' forces were not better armed than the Romans, but they profited from determined leadership and high morale. In one of the crucial battles, at Adrianople in 378, the Goths benefited from greater numbers and destroyed a Roman army and killed Emperor Valens.

In 395 the empire was definitively divided into east and west. Under pressure from the Huns further east, the Visigoths under Alaric invaded Italy in 401, sacking Rome in 410. (The city walls had been greatly improved by Emperor Aurelian in the 270s and had held off Alaric, but eventually Rome was starved into submission.) The sack of Rome was an important sign of change, one with totemic significance for both imperial authority and the position of the pope. Italy was then extensively ravaged by invaders: Goths, Vandals, and Huns.

Although Roman influence continued in the provinces of the Western Empire, it had been fatally weakened. In 409 a Germanic confederacy of Alans, Suevi and Vandals invaded Spain. Political and military links between Rome and much of the empire, including England and Spain, were sundered in the 410s. Lisbon was devastated by the Visigoths in 419 and captured by the Suevi in 469.

Linked to the invasions, there was also political instability within the Roman world, including civil wars. The emperors took refuge at Ravenna further north in Italy, which was protected by marshland and less exposed to attack than Rome. But even Ravenna could not be held and Romulus Augustulus, the last Roman emperor in the Western Empire, was deposed in 476.

THE LEGACY OF ROME

Most archaeological material surviving from the Roman period indicates a society producing and trading far more goods than its Iron Age predecessors. Meanwhile, the human imprint on the environment increased, with the continued clearing of virgin woodland and the dominance over other species seen, for example, by the wiping out of bears in England.

Rome's legacy was important. Although this legacy was much shadowed by 'barbarian' conquest, Roman rule left Latin culture, Christianity, an urban structure, and an experience of unity, as well as the remains of buildings that are not only still impressive but also helped define the imagination of Rome's successors.

The legacy was taken forward but also subtly changed by Byzantium, the Papacy and the Holy Roman Empire, and, to a degree, the subsequent history of Europe reflected struggles over different interpretations of the Roman imperial legacy. This struggle still reaches into the present day; for example, with contrasting views about the place of Russia in Europe and also the extent to which the European Union draws on aspects of the legacy of Rome.

More immediately the legacy of Rome varied very greatly, partly due to the impact of outside attacks. Internal pressures varied, with former Roman officials and military leaders breaking off and creating their own

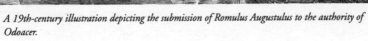
A 19th-century illustration depicting the submission of Romulus Augustulus to the authority of Odoacer.

power bases before and after the fall of the empire, and these then following distinct trajectories. In addition, the experience of the aftermath of the fall of Rome contrasted geographically, economically and culturally. It proved greater for officials, clerics, merchants and townspeople than for peasants.

CHAPTER 3
CENTURIES OF DISRUPTION

*c.*500–1000

The instability of the 5th century hit trade, society and city life hard across the European continent. After the marked population decline of that century, and renewed problems due to disease in the 6th century, there was population growth in both town and country and a significant degree of recovery. However, in the 8th, 9th and 10th centuries there was a second wave of 'barbarian' attacks from peoples including Arabs, Vikings and Magyars. Beginning in the 7th century, the struggle between Islam and Christendom became a major strand in European history.

DARK AGES?

The instability of the 5th and 6th centuries led to a marked sense of crisis and certainly to a feeling of decline from the world of western Roman Christendom. The written record is limited and the archaeological evidence is unevenly spread.

There was undoubtedly a crisis, but at the same time there was both continuity and new development. Italy was no longer the centre of a mighty empire, but some cities survived there, notably Rome, Naples and Ravenna. There was significant development in some places, such as Amalfi, which was relatively protected from attack by land and became an important maritime republic that operated widely in the Mediterranean.

Trade faced far more disruption than it did when under the protection of the Roman Empire. However, it still developed, in both the Mediterranean and also in northern Europe. In part this was a matter of Viking activity, but that was not all. For example, trade between the east coast of England and the Low Countries and the Rhineland was especially important, with wool exports to the continent growing in value.

New developments included the foundation of monasteries, notably those of the Benedictine order founded by Benedict of Nursia in 529. He founded 12 monasteries, firstly Subiaco and most famously Monte Cassino near Rome. The Benedictines became the most significant monastic order and thus set the standard. The life of the monastery was organized in God's service, notably by prayer and work.

A fresco of Saint Benedict of Nursia, who founded the most influential monastic order of the era.

Any summary of the major changes during the Dark Ages has to capture the interplay between the drive for greatness, including unity within a greater whole, and the strength of regional and local particularism. The former drive and unity were presented by Christendom, the Papacy, and the pretensions and hopes focused on the Emperor, and they were to produce a clear consequence in the Crusades that began in the 11th century. This situation, however, left room for tension and disputes, and these drew on the decentralized power structure of feudalism. In addition, the central political questions of dynastic monarchies, the calibre of the ruler and the nature of the succession, ensured a large degree of unpredictability.

Moreover, the rationale and conduct of power were violent. Feuds within and between royal families and within and between tribes ensured that society remained violent, the ethos of heroism being one of glory won through fighting status in England was measured by *wergild*: the different sums payable in disparate social groups as compensation for killing a man.

395–1453	*Byzantine Empire*
450–751	*Merovingian France*
*c.*451–1066	*Anglo-Saxon England*
476–711	*Visigothic Spain*
493–553	*Ostrogothic Italy*
*c.*500–839	*Dal Riata*
567–822	*Avar Khaganate*
*c.*650–969	*Khazar Khaganate*
711–1492	*Al-Andalus*
751–911	*Carolingian Empire*
830–955	*Magyar Hungary*
919–1024	*Ottonian Germany*
882–1240	*Kievan Rus*
900–1286	*Kingdom of Alba*

BYZANTIUM

Divided and in part conquered, the Roman world survived in the eastern Mediterranean, with the Byzantine Empire being the continuation of the eastern Roman Empire. Under Emperor Justinian I (r.527–65) and his talented general Belisarius, between 535 and 555 the Byzantines seized much of Italy, south-east Spain and Tunisia in a series of brilliant campaigns, and also defeated a Frankish invasion of Italy in 554. Spain (in practice south-east Spain) was a province of the Byzantine Empire from 552 to 624.

Behind the mighty Theodosian Walls built around the capital Constantinople in the 440s, Byzantium subsequently held out against Islamic attacks, notably in 674–8 and 717–8. Constantinople finally fell to the Muslim Ottoman Turks under Mehmed II in 1453. However, the earlier advance of Islamic power meant that North Africa and the modern states of Syria, Lebanon, Israel and Palestine were captured by Arab forces in the 7th century. Byzantium was weakened in a bitter and lengthy conflict with the Sassanians of Persia, a conflict that ensured that sufficient resources could not be devoted to preserving Byzantium's new position in the western Mediterranean. The Lombards were to drive the Byzantines from much of Italy, and the Visigoths drove them from Spain. Both Byzantium and Persia were defeated by the Muslim forces, but Byzantium avoided being totally overthrown. Byzantium also repeatedly suffered from internal political conflicts and conspiracies.

At the same time, there were periods of success for Byzantium. A strong leader was the key requirement, as with Justinian (r.527–65) who had also reorganized the legal system. Basil II (r.976–1025) destroyed the Bulgarian empire, a key and longstanding rival that had dominated much of the Balkans from the early 9th century. (Under Symeon of Bulgaria, who died in 927, there had been an assertion of equality with Byzantium.) Basil gained his surname 'Bulgar-slayer' from the Battle of the Belasica Mountains in 1014, after which thousands of prisoners were blinded and sent home in groups of 100, each led by a man blinded in one eye. Bulgaria was annexed in 1018.

In the period 400–1100 Byzantium was the leading state in Christian Europe and an important model for other rulers. It was the centre of

A mosaic of the Byzantine emperor Justinian I, who led a series of campaigns in the 6th century to recover the territory lost when the Western Empire fell.

Orthodox Christianity and both defined and led a different Christendom to that presided over by the Papacy. Descended from churches founded by Christ's Apostles in the 1st century and rooted in Byzantine culture and politics, this was the form of Christianity followed in the Byzantine empire and also in the Balkans and Russia. There is no single Supreme Pontiff equivalent to the Pope.

THE 'BARBARIAN' KINGDOMS

Generally, we do not know how far the so-called barbarian invasions were large-scale movements and how far they were invasions by smaller warrior groups. It was traditionally thought, on the basis of language and place-names, that there had been a mass migration. Then in the 1970s and 1980s, new research placed the emphasis on a small élite invasion. Subsequently, DNA analysis has revived the earlier hypothesis of mass migration.

In Western Europe the 'barbarian' Germanic kingdoms that had succeeded Rome competed with the Franks in France, the Ostrogoths in Italy and the Visigoths in Spain and Portugal, becoming particularly prominent. Theodoric, King of the Ostrogoths, conquered mainland Italy from Odoacer, another 'barbarian,' in 488–92, then Sicily in 493.

Theodoric respected the Roman legacy and restored ancient monuments such as in Ravenna. However, although his kingdom was powerful, it did not last. The Visigoths continued Roman administrative structures and the Latin language, and renounced the Arian heresy, which rejected the Catholic view of the Trinity, in favour of Catholicism. This was a key episode in the establishment of Catholicism and papal authority in the 'barbarian' world.

The 6th-Century Crisis

The 'barbarians' were far from alone in posing a major challenge to the former Roman world. Climate and disease also were highly destructive problems. Analysis of atmospheric pollutants trapped in ice extracted from a glacier in the Swiss-Italian Alps in 2013 suggests that 536 was the beginning of an acute period of crisis and uncertainty. Early that year a volcanic eruption in Iceland spread ash across the whole of Europe. The Byzantine historian Procopius recorded: 'For the sun gave forth its light without brightness, like the moon, during the whole years.' It became very cold and crops failed. In 540 and 547 two similar eruptions occurred. Then in 541 an outbreak of bubonic plague entered Europe from Egypt and went on to kill much of the population of the Byzantine Empire. There were no signs in the column of renewed activity until about 640, when the ice shows a spike of airborne lead, signalling large-scale silver smelting and thus the resumption of some form of organized 'industry'.

The Franks became the dominant figures across much of modern France, Belgium and Germany. They were initially based in the latter two, but in 486 under Clovis (r.481–511), they overthrew the Roman-controlled area under Syagrius in what is now northern France. Clovis also drove the Visigoths from southern France in 507, defeated the Alemanni 'barbarian' group and, by converting to Catholicism, won a degree of legitimation.

As with other 'barbarian' kingdoms, this achievement was jeopardized by division among Clovis' sons. However, the Merovingian dynasty created by Clovis also saw formidable expansion, including the conquest in 534 of Burgundy, another 'barbarian' state which was previously independent, and the conquest of Provence from the Ostrogoths in 537. By the end of the 7th century, disunity within the ruling Merovingian house was matched by growing independence on the part of aristocrats and particularly the 'mayor of the palace' or leading minister.

In the early 8th century Charles Martel, the mayor of the palace, seized power. In 732 at Poitiers he defeated Islamic invaders who had moved north after defeating the Visigoths and conquering Spain and Portugal. His son Pepin III deposed Childeric III, the last Merovingian king in 751 and instead founded the Capetian dynasty. Charlemagne was Pepin's son.

Other 'barbarian' groups included the Suevi in north-west Spain and Portugal, the Burgundians, and the Angles, Saxons and Jutes who invaded and conquered England. There was much conflict among these peoples. The Visigoths conquered the Suevi in the late 6th century. In England the Angles of Northumbria became dominant, especially under Oswy (r.642–70) and Ecgfrith (r.670–85). They were followed in the 8th century by the Angles of Mercia, notably Offa (r.757–96) and in the early 9th century by the Saxons of Wessex. Offa's charters (formal documents) used the term 'King of the English' at least once. Offa is most famous for the construction of an earth dyke frontier line with the Welsh kingdom of Powys that may well have been a defensive work. It must have entailed considerable organization and, along with reforms to coinage, illustrated the administrative capability of Mercian England.

THE ARAB CONQUESTS

Having converted to the new religion of Islam, Arabs shattered existing systems of power across the Middle East, North Africa and Iran, and then sought to spread their influence further. In 711 Arab forces crossed the Strait of Gibraltar and rapidly conquered Spain and Portugal. Christian explanations of the conquest were religious, providential, and moral. The major literary work of the period was the *Commentary on the Apocalypse* by the Spanish monk Beatus. There was a theme of divine judgment in

A late 9th-century ivory plaque shows the baptism of Clovis, the ruler who united the Franks and founded the Merovingian dynasty.

the account of the fall of Visigothic Spain, a story of rape, revenge and betrayal, in which a rape by Roderic, the last king, played a central role. This approach related success against the Muslims to morality, a means that conversely could serve to explain the success of later monarchs. In fact, the internal divisions among the Visigoths, as well as their other military commitments including action against the Basques, played an important part.

Using naval power effectively, Arab forces also conquered the islands in the Mediterranean, from Cyprus to the Balearics, as well as establishing a few bases on its northern shore: most notably in Italy at Bari (841–871) and in France at Fraxinetum (La Garde-Freinet) from 889 to 973. The latter led to raids on the Alpine passes in the early 10th century, which hindered contact between France and Italy. The Muslim advances helped to mould the modern world. This was a cultural as much as a military advance, and one that is a submerged theme in European history. Islamicization would be reversed in relatively few areas, principally Spain, Sicily and the Volga basin.

The Arab Conquest of Sicily

Disunity among Byzantine officials provided the Arabs with an opportunity to establish themselves from 827, although they did not finally conquer the island of Sicily until 965. The Arabs brought citrus fruit, rice and mulberries to Sicily and used slaves to cultivate sugar cane there. Many of the indigenous inhabitants converted to Islam, but divisions among the Arabs enabled the Normans to conquer the island in the late 11th century.

AL-ANDALUS

Schism and division in the Islamic world led to the establishment of an independent Islamic state, the Umayyad emirate, in southern Spain, with its capital from 756 in Córdoba. The most dramatic site, the Great Mosque (*Mezquita*), was begun in the late 8th century and was constructed by demolishing and adapting the church of St Vincent, itself built on the site of a Roman temple dedicated to the god Janus. Most of the Christian population in the Muslim areas eventually adopted Muslim culture and language.

Córdoba's heyday was in the 10th century under Abd al-Rahman III (r.912–61) and his impressive successor as its caliph, Al-Hakam II (r.961–76). The term *convivencia* is frequently used by historians to refer to the multi-ethnic, multi-religious yet supposedly tolerant culture of Al-Andalus. The important Jewish presence there greatly contributed to intellectual life. Al-Hakam II liked books and supported scientific work, encouraging the translation of books from Latin and Greek into Arabic. Arabic mathematical knowledge was also transmitted to Islam. To the north of Spain there were also small Christian principalities. Córdoba declined in the 11th century as a result of division into *taifas,* or separate territories, Christian advances, and invasions from Muslim North Africa. The key defeat of the forces of the Almohad caliph at Las Navas de Tolosa in Andalusia in 1212 was followed by the Christian overrunning of Andalusia in the 1220s and 1230s. This achievement was secured with victory over the forces of the Marinid sultanate of Morocco at the Rio Salado in 1340.

THE FRANKS

The most important 'barbarian' kingdom became that of the Franks, who consolidated control over modern France. The Capetian dynasty proved more successful than the Merovingians, especially under Charlemagne (r.768–814). A great military leader, especially at the expense of the Lombards in Italy and the Saxons in Germany, Charlemagne was also an astute politician. Pope Adrian I had appealed for Charlemagne's assistance against the Lombards, leading to Charlemagne invading Italy in 773. In 774 Charlemagne had himself crowned King of the Lombards. For him there were no limits between 'France' and 'Italy.' He overcame a rebellion in Friuli in 776 and temporarily forced Benevento into submission in 787. Charlemagne's role in Italy proved a major support to the Papacy, not least against rebellion in Rome itself in 799. After thus aligning with the Papacy, on Christmas Day 800 Charlemagne was crowned Emperor

 A 19th-century painting of the court of Abd al-Rahman III.

of the Romans by Pope Leo III, resuming a heritage cut short in 476 and linking the imperial legacy of Rome, the power of the Carolingian empire, and the rising prestige of the Papacy.

Le Chanson de Roland
Under Charlemagne the Franks tried to extend their hegemony to the south of the Pyrenees, but they found it difficult to sustain a presence there, not least as a result of the failure of the 778 campaign to end opposition. The defeat of Charlemagne's rearguard by Basques at Roncevaux Pass in Navarre, as he withdrew following the capture of Pamplona, became a key episode in medieval literature. Charlemagne's biographer Einhard recorded: 'That place is so thoroughly covered with thick forest that it is the perfect spot for an ambush ... the Franks were disadvantaged by the heaviness of their arms and the unevenness of the land.' The 11th century epic poem The Song of Roland *provided a much-embroidered heroic account of this episode.*

Charlemagne's coronation set up two separate European empires, the Carolingians and Byzantium, each claiming the Roman inheritance. His reign was linked with the Carolingian Renaissance, a period of cultural activity that, with his active encouragement, focused on the clergy of Charlemagne's court at Aix-la-Chapelle (Aachen). Schools were founded and textbooks written for them. Workshops produced large numbers of manuscripts including copies of Classical texts. A large number of cathedrals and churches were built in an architectural style that drew on Roman and Byzantine models.

Charlemagne's empire was divided by his heir Louis the Pious among his own sons in 817. Much of Italy went to one son, Lothar, as part of a middle kingdom. Division was entrenched by the Treaty of Verdun (843), which created western, middle and eastern kingdoms, the first the basis for France and the last for Germany. There was then further fragmentation, and also pressure from the Magyars, Vikings and Arabs.

The kingdom of Germany, the eastern kingdom given to Louis' son Louis the German, came to be the key element in the Carolingian inheritance. The Carolingian rulers there came to an end in 911 and were succeeded by the Saxon or Octonian dynasty under Henry I. His son Otto I became king in 936 and added the kingdom of Italy in 951, then defeated the invading Magyars at Lechfeld in 955 and became Holy Roman Emperor in 962. Otto established an effective governmental system that was continued by his successors. This position competed with that of Byzantium, as did the interest of the Emperors in Italy where Byzantium retained an important territorial presence into the 11th century.

THE PAPACY

The authority of the Papacy as head of the Church was asserted, demonstrated and advanced by the coronation of Holy Roman Emperors by the pope. This was an authority consistently defended both against Byzantium, the centre of Orthodoxy, and also against other prelates in the Western Church. In a long-term process, the popes moved from being the foremost of the bishops and, instead, notably under Gregory

At the Battle of Lechfeld in 955, shown here in an illustration from the 15th-century Sigmund Meisterlin *codex, the German army achieved a decisive victory over the Magyar invaders.*

I (r.590–604), claimed primacy. This was to be the basis for subsequent papal attempts to introduce and administer doctrine for the whole of Christendom. Based in Rome, the Popes were determined to make other bishops accept their power as well as authority. This was a matter of prestige, theological control and jurisdictional might.

Byzantium had dominated the Papacy from 537 to 752, appointing the popes or at least approving the choice. Nevertheless, there had been theological conflicts between Byzantium and the popes. From 756 Frankish influence became more significant, with Charlemagne's father,

Pepin III, invading Italy in 754 and 756 in order to provide help for the Papacy against the Lombards.

There was also tension over the authority of Rome in the British Isles. In England this authority was opposed to the Irish-based Celtic Church, but thanks to the support of King Oswy of Northumbria at the Synod of Whitby in 664, Roman authority prevailed. England became an active part of a dynamic cultural world that looked to Rome, although this was based on ecclesiastical and religious links rather than imperial power and its military rationale, as under the Roman Empire.

VIKING EXPANSION

The Vikings, who came from present-day Scandinavia, which was then divided into a number of independent territories, dramatically changed the history of northern Europe, not only transforming the Baltic but also ranging further afield as they searched for opportunities for loot, trade and land. Most famously, with their clinker-built longships, they showed what maritime links and power could achieve. The Vikings permanently expanded Europe by settling Iceland from about 860, although their presence further across the North Atlantic, in Greenland and even more so in Newfoundland and Labrador, proved ephemeral. At the same time the Vikings were more than small-scale warriors. They also saw the development of states that provided a more developed and larger-scale military force. These states were the products of a potent social organization, in which justice mattered and there was considerable equality between men.

The main burden of the Viking attack fell on the British Isles, northern France and the Low Countries. At the same time, they raided in Spain, sacking Seville in 844, and in Italy, sacking Pisa in 860. They were also active across Russia, establishing themselves in Novgorod in 859, and into the Black Sea.

Viking society was very much a warrior one and the sagas that provided its history praised bravery and honour. Vikings proved more effective than most of their opponents and, whereas the 'barbarian' attacks of the 3rd and 4th centuries had seen troops moved from one part of the Roman

Empire to another, no such response was offered to the Vikings.

Initially the Vikings were pagans who violently opposed Christianity and were seen as a destructive scourge by monks in the monasteries they devastated, such as Lindisfarne in England in 793. However, the Vikings were eventually converted. This helped bring Scandinavia into the European mainstream.

Alfred, King of Wessex (r.871–99)
After his kingdom was nearly crushed by Viking attacks in 871 and 877, Alfred reorganized his forces and defeated the Danes at Edington in 878, winning further successes in the 880s and 890s. He strengthened Wessex, fostered an image of Christian kingship that drew on Carolingian examples, patronized learning, founded a navy, and issued a law code. The earlier destruction of the other Anglo-Saxon ruling houses by the Vikings allowed Alfred and his successors to portray themselves as English, rather than merely West Saxon, kings. Alfred's grandson Athelstan conquered the Viking kingdom of York in 927.

In England the conversion of the Vikings followed their defeat in the late 9th century by Alfred, King of Wessex. However, after another major assault under King Cnut of Denmark and his sons, the Vikings ruled England from 1016 to 1042. Cnut also conquered Norway in the 1020s. Danish control contrasted with the impact and consequences of Norman invasion and rule from 1066. Cnut sought to rule, not as a foreign oppressor but as a lord of both Danes and non-Danes. He was the king of a number of kingdoms, not a monarch seeking to enlarge one kingdom. Unlike William the Conqueror, Cnut acted as inheritor of the Old English monarchy and did not have to face rebellions. The Danish period in English history serves as a reminder of unpredictabilities. Cnut's rule can appear as the consequences of the fortuitous combination of a late burst of Viking activity and, in the person of Aethelred the Unready, a weak English defender.

The Vikings who settled in northern France founded the Duchy of Normandy in 911, and became the Normans. From Normandy, they conquered England under William the Conqueror in 1066 and, from there, overran much of Wales. Other Normans took over Sicily and southern Italy. In Scandinavia, Denmark, Norway and Sweden became major kingdoms which, in the 11th century, sought to project their power into the British Isles and to the eastern Baltic.

IRELAND IN THE DARK AGES

Ireland may not have been attacked by the Romans but it was affected by Christianity from the 4th century. Like much of Europe in this period, its culture was a complex mix of influences: pagan and Christian, oral and literate, native and imported. Celtic Christianity was dominated by monasticism, mysticism and elements of syncretism (which combined traditional pagan practices with Christian doctrine), and was spread by traders as far north as the Faroes and Scotland.

From 794 Ireland suffered Viking attacks and from the foundation of Dublin in 841 the Vikings developed permanent coastal bases. Resistance to Viking attacks brought a measure of political consolidation in the Celtic lands including Ireland. However, Ireland did not see the development of a strong state comparable to England. The crucial political level became the subordinate provincial kingdoms: Connacht, Leinster, Meath, Munster and Ulster, each divided in turn into independent lordships based essentially on tribal domains. This led to vulnerability when attacked by Anglo-Norman nobles in the 12th century.

SCOTLAND

During the Roman period, the lands to the north of the Firth of Forth were occupied by the Picts. Their kings displayed their prowess in warfare and hunting, and they kept sacral figures – wizards or shamans – to underline their status. Art of high order, especially carved stones, was produced by this society.

The Picts were affected by the entry of Scots from Ireland into western Scotland, although the scale of movement is unclear. The Scottish kingdom of Dal Riata, with its major seat of power at Dunadd, absorbed the Pictish kingship from 789 and created the new kingdom of Alba from about 900. Historians debate how far Pictish identity was peacefully transmitted into the new polity, and how far violence was involved.

EASTERN EMPIRES

Knowledge of empires in Eastern Europe to the north of Byzantium is limited and essentially a matter of external commentary, in the shape of comments by hostile contemporaries and by modern archaeologists. Three peoples and their empires attract particular attention: the Khazars, Avars and Magyars.

A semi-nomadic Turkic people, the Khazars in the mid-7th century established a wide-ranging empire in the south-eastern part of European Russia that drew its wealth from its commercial position at the western end of the Silk Road. There were no precise boundaries, but the Khazars reached from the Caucasus west into Ukraine and Crimea, and north to the headwaters of the Don, south of modern-day Moscow. Until about 900 Byzantium was an ally. In the late 960s the Khazar empire was destroyed by Kievan Rus, by then an ally of Byzantium.

Further west the Avars, a confederation of steppe people who dominated modern Hungary from the 6th century, were major opponents of Byzantium in the late 6th and early 7th centuries. They were overthrown by Charlemagne in 791 in a major eastward projection of power.

Subsequently, the Magyars, a Finno-Ugric tribe from central Russia, entered Hungary at the close of the 9th century. They assimilated or enslaved the small Hungarian population of the period and from there actively raided west from the late 900s, notably into southern Germany, although they were defeated by Otto I at the Battle of Lechfeld in 955. They underwent a conversion to Christianity at the close of the 10th century. Stephen I was crowned king of Hungary in 1000, with a crown sent by Pope Sylvester II, and established a diocesan structure.

KIEVAN RUS

A major product of the Viking diaspora was the economy, state and culture of Kievan Rus. Developed by Viking traders from the mid-9th century and based in Kiev on the River Dnieper, with an important

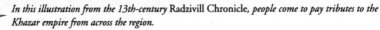

In this illustration from the 13th-century Radzivill Chronicle, *people come to pay tributes to the Khazar empire from across the region.*

base further north at Novgorod, Rus expanded greatly as a territorial power in the mid-10th century. Kievan Rus benefited from dominance of river-borne trade between the Baltic and the Black Sea, from the related links with Byzantium, and from economic links with Central Asia via the Volga Bulgars in the area of Kazan. Links with Byzantium were greatly strengthened by the conversion of the Rus to Greek Orthodox Christianity after 987, a development of crucial significance in European history as it helped give what became Russia a heritage from Byzantium, eventually encouraging the idea that Moscow was the 'Third Rome'. In contrast, Russia was not to look to the Papacy, unlike, for example, Poland.

The Kievan state dissolved after the death of Vladimir I (r.978–1015), who was succeeded by sons who ruled separate principalities based on Novgorod, Polotsk and Chernigov. There was further division after the death of Yaroslav the Wise (r.1019–54). Kiev was sacked by Polvotsy nomads in 1093 and in 1169 by Suzdal, a new principality to the north-east. As a result the title of Great Prince was transferred to the ruler of Suzdal.

CHAPTER 4
THE MIDDLE AGES
1000–1450

The European society, culture and politics of the Middle Ages leaves a potent legacy to the modern day, not least in terms of the states created in that period, from Portugal to Russia. Christendom expanded in Iberia, the Baltic and Lithuania, but lost out to the advance of the Turks in the Balkans. Much of lowland Europe was cultivated and industry and trade developed.

THE CRUSADES

Pressure on Byzantium by the Seljuk Turks led Pope Urban II to call from 1095 for a holy war against Islam that was designed to capture Jerusalem, the most sacred site of Christendom. This led to the First Crusade, with the Christian warriors granted indulgences for their sins in return for their service. Having advanced overland, they captured Jerusalem in 1099 and established a series of Crusader territories, most significantly the kingdom of Jerusalem. But the initial expansion proved difficult to maintain and the pressure on these territories led to subsequent crusades, beginning with the Second Crusade before the loss of Jerusalem to Saladin in 1187. The Crusades eventually failed, with the last major position, Acre (now in northern Israel), falling to the Mamluks of Egypt after a siege in 1291.

1085	*Fall of Toledo*
1094	*Fall of Valencia*
1095	*Council of Clermont*
1096–99	*First Crusade*
1144–55	*Second Crusade*
1147	*Wendish Crusade*

1147–85	*Fall of Lisbon*
1187–92	*Third Crusade*
1198	*Livonian Crusade*
1202–04	*Fourth Crusade*
1209–29	*Albigensian Crusade*
1212	*Battle of Las Navas de Tolosa*
1217–21	*Fifth Crusade*
1228–29	*Sixth Crusade*
1230	*Prussian Crusade*
1236	*Fall of Cordoba*
1248	*Fall of Seville*
1248–54	*Seventh Crusade*
1270	*Eighth Crusade*
1271–2	*Ninth Crusade*
1291	*Fall of Acre*
1492	*Fall of Granada*

The Christians were more successful in the Mediterranean. Islands that had been conquered by the Muslims, notably Crete and Sicily, were regained. In addition, driving back Islam brought a measure of security for other territories.

In northern Europe there were crusades against 'heathens' that also extended German power in the eastern Baltic. There were also crusades against heresy, most particularly against the Albigensians of southern France in the early 13th century.

Military Orders
The Crusaders founded a number of territories in the region and inspired a novel organization that had clear political overtones –

the military orders of knights pledged to defend Christendom. Most of the membership were laymen. The Knights Templar, the largest order, was founded in 1118 and the Knights Hospitaller had troops and castles and were entrusted with the defence of large tracts of territory.

 A contemporary manuscript shows the Battle of Toulouse, a significant engagement in the Albigensian Crusade of the 13th century.

MEDIEVAL RELIGION

Christianity was both dynamic and divided. The key element in the division was the schism between Catholicism and Orthodoxy, formalized in 1054 with a break in communion between the churches. This schism focused on the authority of the pope, which was rejected in Byzantium and Russia, and on liturgical and other differences that had arisen due to the separate systems of theological authorization in Western and Eastern Europe. Meanwhile, proselytism also spread the religion, especially for Catholicism in north-east Europe, which saw a series of Baltic crusades, for example in Latvia, as well as more peaceful proselytizers. Finally, Lithuania, the last major pagan area, was converted in 1386.

Crusades against northern pagans were authorized by Pope Alexander III in the early 1170s, but the Wendish Crusade in north-eastern Germany had begun in 1147, the Danes captured Rugen in 1165 and the Swedes began crusading in Finland in the 1150s. This activity increased in range and scale from the late 12th century, although in practice it drew on long-lasting conflict in the period. Knightly orders were founded to assist the struggle, notably the Teutonic Knights, but they failed in their campaigns against Novgorod in Russia and Lithuania.

However, division was more clearly to the fore in the core areas under Catholicism. Here, clergy owed loyalty to two masters: the pope and the lay ruler. The Roman Catholic church was subject legally and to a large extent in practice to the Papacy. A bitter power struggle between the German-based Holy Roman Empire and the Papacy in Rome repeatedly caused problems, particularly from the Investiture Crisis of the late 11th century onwards. In theory the two were aligned, each as the helper of the other. In practice, a struggle for primary arose from serious differences in Italian power politics, as well as important ideological tensions. On several occasions emperors sponsored 'anti-popes,' such as Honorius II (1061–64) who contested the authority of the pope, while the Popes in turn backed rival imperial claimants. However, the idea of a universal pope and undivided Catholicism was not challenged and on each occasion schism was eventually resolved. Nevertheless, the schisms of the 14th century, which saw rival popes in Rome and Avignon, lasted until 1417.

A New Monastic Energy

The Roman Catholic Church was able to develop monasticism as a more dynamic force. The key and longstanding monastic order, the Benedictine, was supplemented by a number of later orders, notably the French-based Cistercians founded in 1098. They proved particularly adept at founding monasteries in areas of little or no population and developing them economically as part of a more general process of expanding settlement. This was especially true in England and Portugal. Subsequently, the Church tapped into the dynamism represented by the foundation of the new orders of friars, notably the Franciscans, founded by St Francis of Assisi and gaining papal recognition in 1210, and the Dominicans. They followed an active form of ministry as opposed to the withdrawal from the world seen with monasticism.

Assertive popes, notably Gregory VII (r.1073–85), Innocent III (r.1198–1216), and Alexander IV (r.1254–61), disciplined and/or deposed rulers across Europe, including Kings Henry II and John of England, and the Holy Roman Emperors Henry IV and Frederick II. The rapid growth in papal pretensions from the late 11th century came at a time when the papal curia (court), under a succession of lawyer popes, was becoming in effect the legal centre of western Christendom and a prime source of papal authority and money, which led to disputes throughout western Christendom. In the Investiture Crisis, the ambitious and determined Pope Gregory VII united the opponents of Emperor Henry IV (r.1084–1106), which weakened imperial authority. Henry was obliged to show contrition and seek pardon in a famous scene at Canossa in 1077, although this led only to a brief pause in the disputes. The Papacy was backed by most of the communes (towns) in Italy, whereas the emperors tended to be supported by the aristocracy.

Disputes over papal claims helped in the formation of 'proto-national' churches and of a 'national' ecclesiastical consciousness, which often demonstrated hostility to 'foreign' clerics. Papal government also stimulated the development of indigenous government. The rise of national ecclesiastical consciousness was furthered greatly during the Great Schism (1378–1417), which fractured the universalism of papal government. The transfer of the Papacy from Rome to Avignon (1305–77), and the great schism in western Christendom between areas owing allegiance to the rival popes in Rome and Avignon, undermined confidence and stability.

In addition, more specific political issues led to repeated tension. The hostility of successive emperors to the pretensions and Italian interests of the Papacy affected the situation in Germany. Moreover, relations between England and the Papacy were complicated by the hostile English response to the papal position regarding England's conflicts with France and Scotland.

The Roman Catholic Church played a central role in society, not least as the crucial source of education, health and social welfare. Medieval hospitals, for example, were primarily religious institutions, offering warmth, food and shelter, rather than clinical treatment. They provided shelter to lepers and others who would otherwise have been outcasts. Confraternities of the devout (non-ordained) laity also played a key role in social welfare.

Painting

Churches required paintings, while lay patrons also increasingly wanted paintings for themselves. Wealth was channelled into artistic patronage. Key painters included the Italians Cimabue (c.1240–1302) and his pupil Giotto (c.1266–1337), each of whom took forward the representation of the human shape, especially by introducing characterization and individuality. Giotto was an important contributor to the frescoes of the church at Assisi dedicated to St Francis.

Lay piety drew on the strength of popular religion, which was also expressed in the cult of saints and in belief in magic. The role of the dark – a world outside human understanding and control – in the life of the imagination, was the product of a more generalized sense of fear. This was a world of malevolence where the Devil and witches were real as figures in the legions of evil. Traditional religious practices and beliefs were supported by a host of verbal and visual narratives, including carols, mystery plays, stained-glass windows, statues and wall paintings. Lay piety could have a heretical fringe, as with Catharism (the Albigensian heresy) in southern France and, at a smaller scale, Lollardy in England which, following the teachings of John Wycliffe, rejected transubstantiation and papal authority and praying to saints, and focused on the authority of the Bible and on a different account of the Eucharist. Each was stamped out, the former following a crusade in the early 13th century.

Anti-Semitism

Anti-Semitism had existed in earlier centuries, for example in Visigothic Spain in the 7th century, but it saw a rapid increase around the continent of Europe from the 1090s. It reflected a hostility to aliens that became a readily apparent feature of medieval England and was a counterpart to the Crusades. The persecution of non-Christians focused on Jews and was linked to bloody pogroms and to false accusations, notably of child murder. The Jews were expelled from England in 1290, a measure that theoretically remained in force until 1655.

FEUDALISM

Feudalism, the essence of the politics and society of Western Europe after the Dark Ages, rested on a contract, but one expressed in terms of personal loyalty rather than a written document. By swearing homage to their lords men became 'vassals' and were given land. In return for this land they provided military service. Kings were the most powerful lords. They were best able to lead the feudal system in their countries if they were successful in war. In contrast, poor leadership could well prove fatal.

At the same time royal power and state formation were not inherently opposed to feudalism and aristocratic power. Instead, they drew on each other, and aristocratic power could exist within governmental institutions as well as outside it. The tension between these two outcomes was important to the political history of the age.

The entire system rested on labour control in the form of serfdom. This varied in terms of its legal basis, practical implications and context, but in essence it was a system of forced labour based on hereditary bondage to the land. As a result, serfs were bought and sold with the land. Serfdom was used to provide the mass labour force necessary for agriculture. It restricted the personal freedom of humans and in its most severe form was akin to slavery. Serfs were subject to a variety of obligations. For example they had to use their lords' mills, they owed dues on a variety of occasions including marriage and death, and they could be sold.

Castles

Castles were centres of power and symbols of authority that often literally towered over the surrounding city or countryside. They also had clear military value, not least as a symbol of territorial control and expansion. The frequent use of names such as Newcastle, Neuburg and Neufchâteau testified to the significance of new fortifications. Fortification techniques developed over time in terms of enlarging the size and raising the height of castle works, and in increasing their complexity. During the Reconquista in Spain and Portugal, castles were built to secure the conquests from Islamic counter-attacks. They also protected gains from other Christian rivals, as when Portugal built castles at Alcoutim and Castro Marim to resist (Spanish) Castilian pressure. Across Europe cities were also walled, both for defence and also to establish the jurisdiction of the relevant authorities. The walls were often formidable, such as those of Constantinople and Paris.

Feudalism was a constantly changing concept. In place of classic feudalism, in which landed estates were given for military service, this was a system in which lords rewarded their followers and retained their services with an annual payment, rather than with land. The burdens of vassals were quickly commuted into cash. This reflected a number of factors, including the need for money and flexibility and the subdivision of estates given to knights. The initial relationship created by the allocation of land slackened with time and with the impact of hereditary property rights. This relationship altered from that of lord and man to landlord and tenant and lord and client. In addition, some lords preferred to fulfil their military obligations by employing household knights and expecting their tenants to provide money rather than military service. The resulting clientage was dominated by powerful nobles whose willingness to raise troops was crucial to the ability of rulers to field armies. This form of patronage and clientage was not necessarily a cause of civil conflict but in the event of a breakdown in relations between monarch and nobles, or between nobles, it made it easier for nobles to mobilize and sustain their strength.

NORMAN CONQUESTS

In some respects the last stage of the 'barbarian' invaders, the Normans were descendants of those Vikings who settled from 911 in Normandy in northern France and began a process of state-building there. In 1066 Duke William of Normandy ('William the Conqueror') invaded England after the death of Edward the Confessor, claiming that Edward had bequeathed him the throne and that Harold, Edward's successor, was a usurper. William defeated and killed Harold at the Battle of Hastings and, having advanced on London, was acclaimed king of England.

The previous unification of England by the House of Wessex ensured that it fell rapidly to William. Even so, the conquest did not run entirely smoothly and William did not crush the entire Anglo-Saxon élite in 1066; there was a widespread rebellion, especially in the north in 1068–70. England was not really brought under control until the late 1070s.

After 1066 England was part of a state that spanned the English Channel, which found itself obliged to ward off the ambitions of other expanding territories. Normandy had a long land frontier and aggressive neighbours, notably the kingdom of France. The continuous military effort this entailed led the Norman rulers to develop England's government as a source of the necessary revenues.

On the borders with their Celtic neighbours within Britain, the Normans' position was much less well defined. In Wales and Ireland this provided opportunities for Norman adventurers to seize land. The same was true in southern Italy, where Norman adventurers moved from being professional soldiers to seizing power. Robert Guiscard (c.1015–85) established a strong position and his younger brother Roger completed the conquest of Sicily. In turn, Roger II of Sicily (r.1105–54) united southern Italy and Sicily and created a powerful state. Where the Normans seized power they replaced the social élite, but there was no mass displacement of the original population and they retained much of the earlier administrative structure.

In Scotland, in contrast to Wales and Ireland, the existing kings were able to call in Norman aristocratic families for support without having to face an invasion. The fertile central belt was under the control of the Scottish crown, and although Scotland was ethnically diverse it was given political direction and a degree of cohesion by capable rulers, especially David I (r.1124–53).

CITIES AND TRADE

During the Middle Ages cities revived, after being damaged in the 'barbarian' invasions of the 5th and 6th centuries and hit hard by the disruption of economies. Many were independent. In the Mediterranean, Venice, Genoa and Pisa developed into major trading cities. They exploited their increasing maritime strength and established financial networks to become the driving economic force in the region. A similar process was underway in the Baltic cities of the Hanseatic League, a confederation developed in the late 12th century. Of these, Lübeck was the most significant. These cities organized widespread networks of trade and a few, notably Venice and Genoa, also developed as significant territorial powers. Thus, at various times Genoa controlled Liguria, Corsica and Sardinia, as well as islands in the Aegean. Venice expanded greatly in the early 15th century, partly at the expense of other cities that it took over, notably Padua (1405), Verona (1405) and Brescia (1426).

An illustration of Venice in the 13th century from an illuminated manuscript. The city became a hub for trade during the Middle Ages.

THE HOLY ROMAN EMPIRE IN THE MIDDLE AGES

Germany, Italy and the imperial status combined in the Holy Roman Empire, the legacy of Charlemagne's prestige, to create the major political presence and force west of Byzantium. However, the empire was a system of prestige rather than a state. The Ottonian (919–1024) and then Salian dynasties of emperors were succeeded by the Hohenstaufen dynasty in the person of Conrad III (r.1138–52). The dynasty, which dominated Western Europe in the late 12th and early 13th century, bringing the medieval Empire to a height, was named after the Swabian castle of Staufen. The most significant emperors of that dynasty, Frederick I (r.1152–90) and Frederick II (r.1220–50), faced opposition from German princely rulers, the Papacy and Italian opponents, notably the Lombard cities.

Nicknamed 'Barbarossa' or Redbeard, Frederick (r.1152–90) was the second of the Hohenstaufen emperors. Succeeding his uncle, Conrad III, he was a vigorous ruler but his position was affected by the growing power of many of the leading aristocratic families, especially the Guelphs in Saxony. Henry the Proud, the head of the Guelphs, had resisted Conrad III and his son, Henry the Lion, Duke of Saxony and Duke of Bavaria, was a crucial figure in Barbarossa's reign. After he broke with the emperor in 1176 he was deprived of his lands in 1180 and exiled. Frederick was committed to maintaining and expanding imperial power in Italy, where he led six expeditions from 1154, being defeated at Legnano in 1176 by the Lombard League. This weakened his position in Germany, although the extent of Hohenstaufen territory there remained considerable. He drowned while on the Third Crusade.

Frederick II was keen on the arts and on intellectual life, and founded the University of Naples. He spoke six languages, including Arabic, and had Arab, Greek and Jewish scholars in his court. He helped introduce Arab and Greek science into Italy, and Europe more generally, and developed early Italian vernacular language and literature.

Frederick II's grandson, Conradin, was defeated and executed in 1268 by Charles of Anjou, brother of Louis IX of France who had been made King of Sicily by the Pope. This ended the Hohenstaufen state in southern Italy, but in 1282 Sicily rebelled and drove out Charles, instead turning to the House of Aragon, the rulers of eastern Spain. The commitment of so much effort repeatedly to Italian struggles had weakened the imperial position in Germany.

RUSSIA, EASTERN EUROPE AND THE MONGOL CONQUESTS

The wide-ranging conquests of the Mongols under Chinggis Khan (c.1160–1227) and his successors affected much of Eurasia including Eastern Europe. The Europeans were never able to defeat the Mongols and were lucky that Chinggis had concentrated on China and then Central Asia. However, the situation changed from the early 1220s when a Mongol force invaded Crimea and defeated the Russians at the Kalka river north of the Sea of Azov. More seriously, in the late 1230s the challenge resumed and Russian principalities were overrun.

Major centres fell as Mongol siege engineers weakened the value of defensive works, such as at the strongly fortified city of Riazan, which was successfully stormed in 1237 after a relief army had been defeated by the Mongols. In 1238 and 1239 many other cities fell, including Suzdal and Kiev. No city appeared safe.

In 1241 the Mongols successfully invaded Poland and Hungary. Crossing the frozen River Vistula, the Mongols sacked Cracow and pressed on into Silesia, defeating a Polish-German army at Leignitz where the horns of the Mongol forces outflanked their opponents. They pressed on to defeat the Hungarians at Mohi. Buda fell soon after. Mongol invaders of Europe only turned back when news arrived of the death of the Great Khan.

The Mongols developed existing links along the 'Silk Roads', which became a key source of new ideas and products entering Europe, such as gunpowder from China in the mid-13th century. The Europeans were far less successful in projecting influence eastwards.

996	*Adoption of Christianity in Poland*
1000	*Kingdom of Hungary established*
1091	*Independence of Serbia*
1097	*Union of Hungary and Croatia*
1102	*Hungarian acquisition of Dalmatia*
1138–1320	*Polish Period of Fragmentation*
1180–4	*Hungarian-Byzantine War*
1223	*Battle of the Kalka River*
1237	*Mongols conquer Ryazan*
1239	*Mongol conquest of Kiev*
1241	*Mongol Invasion of Poland and Hungary*
1241	*Battle of Leignitz*
1370	*Union of Hungary and Poland*
1384	*Death of Louis the Great, end of Polish-Hungarian union*
1385	*Union of Poland and Lithuania*

The key states in Eastern Europe were Hungary and Poland, but their strength and stability varied greatly. There were also lesser states, such as Serbia, that were able to influence developments. Poland became a major state from the late 10th century, with its recognition by the Germans helped by its conversion to Christianity. However, the strength of the Polish monarchy was gravely affected by the rise in the power of the greater nobility and by the granting of provinces to members of the ruling Piast dynasty. Boleslaw III (r.1102–38) divided Poland between his sons in his will, which made it difficult to resist the rise of the nobles or German expansion, and this 'period of fragmentation' lasted until 1320. In contrast, Hungary expanded considerably in the late 12th century, especially into southern Croatia, Bosnia and Wallachia, while, in the 1180s both Serbia and Bulgaria gained independence from Byzantium and each expanded greatly at the expense of Byzantium.

The massive disruption of Mongol invasion was followed by the establishment of tributary states in Russia and new dynasties in both Hungary and Poland. Each found it difficult to control their nobility and also had to confront the complex power politics of the period. There were no obvious territorial boundaries for these or other states. The Angevin rulers of Hungary oversaw a great territorial expansion in the mid-14th century and in 1370 Louis the Great of Hungary also succeeded the childless Casimir the Great as king of Poland. This amalgamation, however, was not long to survive the death of Louis in 1382, which was an indication of the essentially transient nature of state-building, especially in Eastern Europe. Louis' authority had reached from the Adriatic to the Black Sea, from the Serbian valley of the Vardar to the frontier of Prussia, but there was no political, strategic, economic, geographical or ethnic logic to such a conglomeration, and no real constituency of interest or opinion behind it.

Louis had no sons and divided his inheritance among his two daughters. The marriage of Hedvig to the Lithuanian Jagiello united Poland and Lithuania, a union that lasted until the late 18th century and helped anchor Lithuania, which had expanded greatly in the chaos after the Mongol invasions, within Catholic Europe. Louis' other son-in-law,

Sigismund (r.1387–1437), was successful in uniting Hungary, Bohemia, the position of Holy Roman Emperor, and some important possessions in that empire. However, he proved unable to overcome the Hussite rebellion in Bohemia and his family's position in the Empire was to be taken by that of the rising Austrian family of Habsburg, who had taken over Austria in the late 13th century. In 1438 Albert II of the House of Habsburg became Holy Roman Emperor and this position was then held by the Habsburgs, with one short break, until 1806.

THE *RECONQUISTA*

Islamic conquest of Spain and Portugal in the early 8th century was followed by a long process of *Reconquista*, or reconquest. The Christians had far more success in Spain and Portugal than in the Near East. The *Reconquista* gathered pace in the late 11th century with the capture of Toledo in 1085 and Valencia in 1094. However, intervention from North Africa, first from the Almoravids (1060s) and then the Almohads (1150s), lent new energy to Muslim resistance. The 12th century saw significant Christian gains. An independent Portugal expanded greatly with the capture of Lisbon in 1147, a capture to which English crusaders greatly contributed.

In the early 13th century the *Reconquista* gathered pace again, recovering the energy that had been shown in the late 11th century. In 1212 Alfonso VIII of Castile, commanding the united armies of Castile, Aragôn, Navarre and Portugal, crushed the caliph at Las Navas de Tolosa. This was to be the crucial and lasting victory of the *Reconquista*, and was understood at the time as a key success.

Most of southern Spain was overrun by 1275, including Córdoba (1236) and Seville (1248). Faro, the last Islamic position in Portugal, fell in 1249 and Granada, the last in Spain, in 1492. These wars helped define the societies and cultures of large areas. Islamic sites were destroyed or converted. Mosques became churches, often, as at Faro, a return to their earlier function. In Córdoba a cathedral was built inside the great mosque. Muslims were driven out or reduced to being serfs and slaves. In time the practice of Islam was forbidden. The *Reconquista* produced militant Christian societies.

UNIFYING FRANCE

The last Carolingian king, Louis V, died in 987. In his place Hugh Capet was elected, inaugurating the Capetians as the new ruling dynasty in France, which was to last more than 800 years. However, the leading nobles won greater autonomy for themselves. By the end of the 10th century the king's domain was essentially confined to the Île de France, the area around Paris. Elsewhere, the counties and courts ceased to be public institutions and local official posts were absorbed into the patronage systems of the greater nobles. Counts wielded governmental powers: they minted coins, raised troops and built castles. The counties did not seek to replace the king: they scarcely needed to do so. Some were themselves as powerful as the king. This was particularly so once the Duke of Normandy became King William I of England in 1066, and after the marriage of Henry II (r.1154–89) of England (also ruler of Normandy, Maine and Anjou) to Eleanor of Aquitaine brought him control over most of southern France.

However, the following century saw a great expansion in the royal domain in France, the part directly under the king. The determination and military success of Philip Augustus (r.1180–1223) led to King John of England losing Normandy and Anjou in 1203–4 and failing to secure their reconquest. John's son, Henry III (r.1216–72), also failed to regain these lands and lost Poitou as well. His successors, Edward I (r.1272–1307) and Edward II (r.1307–27), focused on an unsuccessful attempt to subjugate Scotland.

MAGNA CARTA AND THE RISE OF PARLIAMENT

Defeat by France and misgovernment produced a crisis of unpopularity for King John (r.1199–1216) and this led in 1215 to what was later called *Magna Carta*, a charter of liberties forced from the king by baronial opponents in the form of a limitation in written form of royal rights with royal power placed under the law.

Although Parliament was not mentioned in the document, *Magna Carta* was an important stage in its development, in particular by linking taxation to consent. Moreover, Parliament turned out to be a pathway to constitutional government that was more effective than the issuing of

Hugh Capet established the Capetian dynasty in France in 987.

charters by a monarch. Under Henry III (r.1216–72), shire knights began to be elected to Parliament and selected towns sent representatives. The institutional practices and pretensions of Parliament were established and elaborated, and the frequent need to raise taxation to pay for warfare led to Parliament becoming more important. This helped to differentiate the English Parliament from its continental counterparts. In addition, Parliament was the representative assembly of the entire kingdom and not a part of it.

INDEPENDENT SCOTLAND

Scotland preserved its independence after major struggles. From the late 12th to the late 13th century the monarchs spread their power out from the central lowlands, extending their control in Galloway, Moray, Argyll, Ross, Caithness and the Western Isles. Broader social, economic and cultural developments also contributed to a measure of cohesion. The notion of 'Scotland' became stronger as patterns of behaviour associated with the royal heartland spread into other areas. The formation of a distinctively Scottish Church also contributed to a developing sense of national identity. Alexander II (r.1214–49) was unsuccessful in exploiting English divisions to pursue Scottish claims to Northumberland, Cumberland and Westmorland, but the Canmore dynasty reached its zenith under Alexander III (r.1249–86). He was succeeded by three-year-old Margaret, the Maid of Norway. She was contracted to marry the future Edward II, which would have led to a union with the English crown, but she died in 1290. Edward I of England then sought to dominate Scotland but faced serious resistance from the 1290s. In 1314 Robert Bruce, Robert I of Scotland, routed Edward II at Bannockburn and in 1328 the Treaty of Northampton-Edinburgh recognized Scottish independence and Bruce's kingship.

THE HUNDRED YEARS' WAR

Conflict between England and France resumed with the outbreak of the Hundred Years' War in 1337, which saw King Edward III of England (r.1327–77) claim the French throne. The fortunes of the ensuing war were mixed, but the use of longbowmen helped to bring the English victory at Crécy (1346) and Poitiers (1356), leading to the Peace of Brétigny (1360). In this agreement Edward promised to renounce his claim to the French throne, Normandy and Anjou, but was recognized as Duke of Aquitaine and ruler of the port of Calais, which had been captured in 1347. However, control over Aquitaine proved difficult to maintain and the English were soon driven from much of it. This was a reminder of the highly changeable nature of political fortunes in this period.

The English did not regain the initiative until Henry V (r.1413–22) invaded France in 1415. At the Battle of Agincourt his longbowmen blunted the successive advances of the French, with very heavy losses. Henry was also helped by powerful support from within France, as the

 The Magna Carta, *signed in 1215, put limits on monarchical power.*

conflict was in part an international dimension to a French civil war, notably between the Dukes of Orléans and Burgundy. The conflict was also influenced by international relations in the Low Countries, Germany and Iberia. Henry's conquest of Normandy in 1415–17 was followed by King Charles VI of France's betrothal of his daughter Catherine to Henry, and by his being recognized as Charles' heir. Henry wished to absorb the leadership of Christendom in so far as it was held by the French. This played a role in the anxiety of Parliament about keeping the two crowns separate and not becoming a satellite of France.

However, Charles VI's son the Dauphin (Charles VII from 1422) continued to resist. The English had some success until 1429, when

 The Battle of Poitiers in 1356 was an important English victory in the Hundred Years' War and the French king John II was captured.

Charles was energized by the charismatic Joan of Arc, who ensured that the English siege of Orléans failed. As the balance of military advantage shifted the English lost political support and the French captured Normandy and Gascony between 1449 and 1451, then defeated an English counter-attack in 1453. Though still claiming the French throne, the English were left holding only Calais, which was lost in 1558. The claim to the French throne was only abandoned in 1802, but the Norman duchy, the Angevin empire and Lancastrian France had all gone.

This failure did not check England's sense of national consciousness. In fact, English involvement in France had arguably forwarded, rather than delayed, the development of a national state, encouraging xenophobia, royal war propaganda, military service, national taxation, and the related expansion of the role of Parliament. As on other occasions, war had helped create a sense of 'us' and 'them,' a sense that was important to English identity. A pre-Reformation 'national' church had also crystallized, against a background of papal claims and of royal and other resistance to them.

Overlapping jurisdictions, a cross-border aristocracy and England's peace within the Plantagenet amalgamation of distinctive territories had all inhibited the development of a national consciousness. Therefore, when it came, the total defeat of the attempt on the French throne in the Hundred Years' War was highly significant. The loss of the French empire of the kings of England helped make England different from the continental dynasties, notably the Habsburgs, Valois, Aragonese and Vasa, that sought to create far-flung territorial empires across Western Europe.

The Origins of Switzerland

The successful Swiss defiance of Habsburg rule from the late 13th century led to the establishment of a confederation of autonomous cantons in 1389, following major victories at Morgarten (1315) and near Zug (1386). William Tell, a fictional figure, symbolizes the struggle for independence. In the 14th and 15th centuries the confederation rapidly expanded, especially to the south-east, north-east and west. Some of these gains proved temporary but the fighting ability of the Swiss infantry proved crucial to their success. In 1499 the Swiss were to force the Emperor Maximilian to acknowledge their effective independence, a reward for their determination.

THE SPREAD OF THE MARKET ECONOMY

From the 10th to the 14th centuries agricultural prosperity was helped by a rising population, which provided markets and workers, as well as by improved technology, including the introduction of windmills from the 11th century. The spread of water-powered mills also helped to develop corn milling. There was a switch from oxen to the faster and more adaptable (although costlier) horses for ploughing. In parts of Europe including England, large-scale field cultivation of legumes (such as beans and peas) began in the 13th century, which enriched the soil and provided fodder. The wealthy found it easier to benefit from these changes than independent peasant proprietors, many of whom were hit by problems and reduced to subordination.

There was also commercialism linked to increased agricultural production for market, particularly with the shift to sheep-rearing for wool for the cloth industry. This was Europe's leading industry and was found across the continent, particularly in northern Italy, Belgium (notably the cities of Bruges and Ghent) and eventually in England. Sheep-rearing produced benefits for the landowners and merchants involved.

There were also differences between regions. For example, expanding trade and the development of local industries, notably textiles and metallurgy, made northern Italy an advanced economic region. Southern Italy, by contrast, stagnated and increasingly became a source of foodstuffs and raw materials for the cities of the north, which, notably Genoa and Venice, controlled its external trade.

Society became more complex as the distribution of wealth broadened. Monetary transactions, the volume of the currency, domestic and foreign trade, specialization in occupations, social mobility and literacy all increased, and industry spread into some rural areas.

In rural society the key development was from paying rent in services or goods to paying rent with money. This was crucial to the spread of the market economy. In warfare, feudal service was replaced by paid professional soldiers. The management of money became more significant for landowners, institutions and governments, which rewarded expertise and professionalism. Across Europe as a whole, capitalist practices both spread and became more sophisticated.

THE BLACK DEATH AND SOCIETY

The Black Death (1348–50) was a terrible outbreak of plague which spread westward along the Silk Roads, carried by fleas transported by black rats and by the fleas and lice on humans. Genoese merchants fleeing the Mongol advance into Crimea brought the disease back to Europe; first to Sicily, probably by rat fleas living on black rats on their boats. In early 1348 the disease reached northern Italy and from there it spread rapidly.

Other factors influencing the devastating effect of the plague included the pressure of living standards from the increase in population, and the longer-term impact on agricultural productivity and general health from the persistent turndown in the climate known as the 'Little Ice Age', which continued into the 18th century. Temperatures fell, which had a major impact on food yields as the growing season for crops shortened, and the glaciers (modestly) advanced.

As a result of the Black Death an estimated 30–60 per cent of the population of Europe died, with the higher percentage being found in cities. In Florence nearly 60 per cent of the population fell victim to the plague in 1348. The European population remained relatively depressed, before increasing again in the 16th century. Labour shortages were a major result. Land was abandoned, villages deserted, and agricultural production fell, putting a strain on revenues.

The massive fall in population led to acute labour shortages, but these had very different consequences. Whereas in Eastern Europe these shortages encouraged the spread of serfdom, in Western Europe efforts to increase control over the peasants failed. Instead, the shortage of labour gave the peasants the chance to force the abandonment of serfdom.

The Plague of Florence, an early 19th-century illustration of the Black Death, after the description by Giovanni Boccaccio. In Florence more than half the population lost their lives to the plague.

THE OTTOMAN ADVANCE

The Ottoman state originated as a frontier principality in the frontier zone of north-western Anatolia. In the 14th century the Ottomans became an important power on either side of the Sea of Marmara, between the Black Sea and the Aegean Sea. In 1361 they captured Adrianople (Edirne) and moved their capital there in 1402. Christian states appeared powerless in the face of the relentless tide of Ottoman advance and Bulgaria rapidly succumbed. In 1385 Sofia fell to the Turks, followed by Nish in 1386. The apparently inexorable advance of the Ottoman Turks starkly demonstrated the weakness of Christian resistance.

The crisis then escalated. In 1389 the Serbian army of King Lazar was defeated by the Ottomans at Kosovo, breaking the back of Serbian resistance. Serbia and Wallachia became Ottoman vassal states, Constantinople was blockaded, and Thessaly in Greece was conquered. In 1396 a Hungarian-French crusade sent to relieve the Byzantines was destroyed at Nicopolis on the Danube. Western cavalry, many from France, advanced impetuously through the Ottoman infantry, only to be broken on the Ottoman gun lines, then driven back and routed by the Ottoman cavalry reserve. Eastern Christendom appeared doomed.

The remaining fragments of Byzantium were only saved by the far greater success of the Central Asian conqueror Timur the Lame (Tamburlane) in crushing the Ottomans near Ankara in 1402, just as, earlier in the 13th century, Mongol victories over their Arab opponents had delayed the fall of the surviving Crusader positions in the Middle East.

Sultan Murad II (r.1421–44 and 1446–51) restored the Ottoman position, although his siege of Constantinople in 1421 failed. In the 1430s Murad overran much of the Balkans and annexed Serbia in 1439. In 1443, in response to Ottoman successes, a crusade set out under the leadership of Wladislas I of Hungary (Wladyslaw III of Poland). Initially the crusaders captured Nish and Sofia and in 1444 advanced as far as Varna on the Black Sea. However, they were routed and Wladislas was killed there by Murad II, who played a major role in the battle. In 1448 Murad went on to defeat a Hungarian-led crusader army at Kosovo. This ended any hopes of saving Constantinople.

Mehmed II (r.1444–6 and 1451–81) captured Constantinople in 1453, benefiting from superior numbers and the skilful use of artillery. He also overran the Morea (Peloponnese) and some of the Aegean islands. The Ottoman siege of Belgrade in 1456 was raised just as that of 1440 had failed; but Serbia was formally annexed in 1458, Wallachia became a subject principality, Bosnia was conquered in 1463, and Albania was finally conquered in 1478–9.

In 1480 Ottoman forces landed at Otranto in southern Italy, within campaigning distance of Rome. The western Roman Empire had been extinguished just over a millennium earlier, and a new conquest of Western Europe appeared imminent.

THE RISE OF MUSCOVITE POWER

After the Mongol conquests, European Russia was dominated by the Golden Horde, a Mongol successor state which imposed tribute on the Russian principalities and raided them for slaves. However, after the Horde was weakened by Timur (Tamburlane), it divided. This provided opportunities for the principalities and notably for Muscovy. The fall of Constantinople in 1453 enabled Russia to claim the leadership of Orthodox Christianity and this encouraged the policy of 'gathering of the lands of Rus'. In 1456, at Staraia Rusa, the Grand Prince Vassily II of Muscovy was able to defeat an army from the powerful city state of Novgorod that was strong in lancers, by making good use of mounted archers, in part provided by Tatar auxiliaries. As a result, Novgorod was forced to accept Muscovite dominance, an important step in the consolidation of Christian Russia. The city was to be eventually captured in 1477, partly because Grand Prince Ivan III was able to take advantage of its social and political divisions. Other Russian principalities were subjugated and brought under control in the 1450s and 1460s.

CHAPTER 5
RENAISSANCE AND
REFORMATION
1450–1650

Much that appears familiar to us today can be seen in the 15th to 18th centuries, such that it is known as the 'early-modern' period, although that can involve underplaying links with the medieval centuries. International voyages of exploration, the Renaissance and the Reformation, all led to a world in which Western Europe was more dynamic, with its traders and power reaching around the world by 1650.

EXPLORING THE OCEANS

The Portuguese conquered Ceuta in Morocco in 1415, then sailed south along the Atlantic coast of North Africa hoping to discover the sources of the gold brought there from across the Sahara, and to find Prester John, a mythical Christian leader derived from the Christians of Ethiopia, with whom they planned to liberate the Holy Land from Islam. By the 1440s they had reached the Guinea coast and by the 1480s the mouth of the River Congo.

Europeans were increasingly grasping the size and shape of the wider world. On behalf of Portugal, Bartolemeu Dias rounded the Cape of Good Hope in 1488, following a new route into the Indian Ocean. A fellow Portuguese navigator, Vasco da Gama, reached Calicut (Kozhikode today) in 1498 at the end of the first all-sea journey from Europe to India. With their heavier cannon, his ships overcame resistance from Indian ships.

Portugal founded a naval commercial empire in the Indian Ocean. Long-distance trade produced profit but also required financial outlays, which led to the development of distinctive Western practices in trade, eventually including joint-stock companies. Trading bases were established further afield, notably at Macao in China and Nagasaki in Japan. Burgeoning transoceanic expansion left a legacy of magnificent buildings, such as the marvellous Jéronimos monastery in Belém in Lisbon.

Prince Henry the Navigator (1394–1460)

The third son of King John I and a key figure in Portugal's overseas expansion, Henry did not actually sail any further than Morocco. Instead, in part in order to pursue conflict with the Moors, Henry exploited his control over the Order of Christ to finance expansion and also tried to focus navigational expertise. To that end he founded a navigation school at Sagres in 1416. Under Henry, Portuguese navigation discovered the pattern of Atlantic trade winds. Having encouraged the capture of Ceuta in 1415, Henry sought, with the help of his brother Edward (r.1433–8), to find the West African sources of the caravans that brought gold there. Deeply religious, he was celibate and died in debt. He was given the title 'Navigator' later on.

In the papal division of the New World in 1493, followed by the Treaty of Tordesillas in 1494, Portugal gained Africa, the Indian Ocean and what was to be 'discovered' as Brazil, while Spain gained the rest of the Americas. In 1529, the Treaty of Saragossa drew a similar line across the east of Asia. Portugal and Spain had also seized and settled the islands of the eastern Atlantic – the Canaries, Madeira, the Azores, and the Cape Verde Islands, which served as important stopping places on the routes to the West Indies and South America. Gran Canaria was finally subdued by the Castilians in 1483 and Tenerife in 1496, whereas the Azores were uninhabited.

Technological innovations played a key role in European exploration. The use of the compass for navigation by Westerners had begun in the

12th century. Initially nothing more than a needle floating in water, it developed into a pivoted indicator and by the 15th century a compass could compensate for the significant gap between true and magnetic north, making it easier for travellers to fix direction.

The growth of Western trade was challenged by piracy, both European and non-European. Turkish naval power also threatened the Western position in the Mediterranean and contested the advance into the Indian Ocean. However, Europeans were successful in a series of battles in both, notably at Lepanto in 1571, and also put more effort into long-distance trade.

The Columbian Exchange

The creation of the Atlantic world entailed the flow of people and produce from each side of the Atlantic. The Americas produced plants including the potato, the tomato, tobacco and cranberries. The Old World provided diseases, notably smallpox, that hit hard at the native American population, as well as the horse and the gun.

THE RENAISSANCE

More than art was at stake during the Renaissance, which, after earlier anticipations, gained momentum in northern and central Italy in the 15th century. An important impetus was the revival of knowledge of and interest in Classical (Greek and Roman) literature by Humanist scholars. Scholars and writers increasingly used philology (the study of language) as a tool to provide accurate Classical texts and to understand them. This revival delivered new information on the ancient world and, more significantly, models for understanding more recent times and the current situation. Humanistic learning was linked to a self-consciously critical reading of sources. There was a transformation of the Western understanding of time; Renaissance thinkers sought to reach beyond an allegedly decrepit and degenerate present in order to grasp the reality of a more virtuous past. This classification of time presented a distinction that was not present in Christian thought, with its emphasis on a fallen mankind awaiting redemption through a Second Coming of Christ. Instead, history could be inserted into the account in order to distinguish between a 'dark age' and an earlier antiquity that offered the possibility of a renewal, both now and in future. In 1345 the poet Francesco Petrarch (1304–74), the first of the major Italian Humanists, discovered Cicero's *Letters to Atticus*, a key part of the process of discovering lost Classical texts and of drawing attention to them.

The artistic centre of the Renaissance was northern and central Italy, notably the cities of Florence, Venice and Rome. Princely courts such as Mantua and Urbino were also significant. Painting, statuary and architecture were all important areas of activity. The accurate representation of humans proved particularly important to the first two. Michelangelo and Leonardo da Vinci were key figures, creating some of the most memorable works of the period such as the *David* sculpture by the former and the *Mona Lisa* painting by the latter. There was also a Northern Renaissance, notably in Bruges and Ghent in Belgium. The key figure in this was Desiderius Erasmus (1469–1536), a Dutch Humanist who edited the New Testament. Other northern European cities that were major cultural centres included Augsburg in Germany.

 Michelangelo's The Creation of Adam, *painted between 1508 and 1512 on the ceiling of the Sistine Chapel, is one of the many impressive artistic works created during the Renaissance.*

> ### Galileo
>
> *Many of the tendencies of intellectual enquiry seen in the Renaissance continued afterwards but met with increasing opposition. Galileo (1564–1642) was Professor of Mathematics at Padua and then mathematician to Grand Duke Cosimo of Tuscany and was a self-conscious rationalist as well as an empirical researcher into the solar system. Basing his work on the newly-invented telescope, Galileo helped make relevant and convincing the ideas of Nicolaus Copernicus (1473–1543), notably that the Earth moved around the Sun. In doing so Galileo fell foul of the Catholic Church.*

PRINTING

In about 1439 Johannes Gutenberg began using his first printing press in Mainz, Germany. A goldsmith, he took existing techniques and machines (notably the technique of engraving the reversed letter in the mould and the metal punch and presses) and created a system of printing using individual letters that could be moved and re-used. He benefited from the limited number of characters in Western language, in contrast to China, and from the availability of information about the properties of tin, lead and antimony, the metals used for type.

The first printing press was introduced to Italy in 1464–5 and by 1500 there were presses in 236 towns in Europe. By 1600 over 392,000 separate titles had been published in Europe. Major centres of printing eventually included Venice, Lyons, Nuremberg and Antwerp. Printers had to focus on the search for profit, but this did not prevent them from playing a role in fostering a degree of change that helped usher in a different world. This was especially so with the Protestant Reformation, which depended heavily on the power of printed publications to overcome traditional constraints on discussing and spreading ideas. In addition, the printing of the Bible made print a more authoritative source of information. Although printing was a key form of intellectual and cultural transmission, at the same time it created huge social and geographical contrasts, notably in literacy.

THE ITALIAN WARS

The French invasion of 1494 launched what were to be called the Italian Wars. These reflected not only the divisions of Italy, but also a new, or rather renewed, willingness of outside rulers to intervene. Charles VIII of France (r.1483–1498) conquered and laid claim to Naples in 1495, which aroused opposition within Italy and from two powerful rulers who had their own ambitions to pursue: Maximilian I (r.1508–1519), the Holy Roman Emperor, and Ferdinand II of Aragon (r.1479–1516), ruler of Aragon, Sicily and Sardinia, and husband of Isabella of Castile. The resulting rivalry led to a series of conflicts and major battles, notably the defeat and capture of Francis I of France by Charles at Pavia in 1525. The wars, which weakened the Christian response to the Turkish advance, only finally finished in 1559. Italian rulers had to adapt to the wishes of the outsiders and the Medici only re-established their position in Tuscany thanks to the support of Charles. Eventually in 1559 Spain and France agreed, via the Treaty of Cateau-Cambrésis, that Philip II of Spain (great-grandson of Maximilian, Ferdinand and Isabella) would control Milan and Naples and thus that Habsburg Spain would dominate Italy, including the Papacy.

CHARLES V, THE FIRST 'GLOBAL' MONARCH

In 1519 Charles I of Spain, the heir of Aragonese, Castilian, Habsburg and Burgundian inheritances, was elected as the Holy Roman Emperor Charles V. This brought him an unprecedented range of power and pretensions, especially because his Spanish subjects were planting his flag in the Americas, which was to be a source of great wealth. Thanks to the scope of his power, Charles V was able to draw on Italian and German financial and mercantile networks. Their availability ensured that it was possible to exploit Spanish transoceanic expansion using more than just the 'smash-and-grab' practices that featured in the early stages of conquest. German and Italian interests gained protection through co-operation with Spain.

However, Charles faced three persistent challenges; from France, the Turks and the Reformation. Initially he also faced opposition in Spain, where there were risings in 1519–21 against his use of the French language and of non-Spanish advisors, his demands for new taxes, and his disruption of existing patronage networks. By winning over the nobility, Charles crushed these protests.

Charles' ambitions focused heavily on honour and glory, and like his predecessors he put great emphasis on prestige and rank. His search for reputation played a major role in the choices he made, including how he

 Charles V was the most powerful ruler of his era. Reigning over the Holy Roman Empire and Spain, his territories provided him with great wealth and substantial military forces.

resolved the conflicting priorities of his many dominions. Alongside the issues of family interest and personal will, there was also the deployment of the collective power of the many dominions Charles ruled.

As protector of the Catholic Church against Protestants and Muslims, and its propagator in the New World, Charles V presented the new global role for the Spanish monarchy that was begun by his grandparents, Ferdinand of Aragon and Isabella of Castile. This role is illustrated in the *Sala de Audiencias* in the palace in Seville, where a *retablo*, or altarpiece, by Alejo Fernandéz shows the Virgin of the Navigators spreading her protective mantle over the *conquistadors*, their vessels and Charles. Elsewhere, the grandiloquent Latin inscription above the entrance to the royal mausoleum in the Escorial palace built near Madrid by Charles' son Philip II called Charles 'the most exalted of all Caesars'. After the death of King Louis of Hungary at Turkish hands at the battle of Mohács in 1526, Charles' brother Ferdinand was elected King of Bohemia and, more contentiously, advanced a claim to the crown of Hungary.

Charles appeared to have succeeded in forwarding his interests in the late 1540s, having defeated the German Protestant princes, most notably at the Battle of Mühlberg in 1547. However, the situation deteriorated markedly in 1552 as many of the Protestant princes successfully co-operated with Henry II of France in attacking Charles. Soon after, a worn out Charles divided his empire between his brother, Ferdinand I, the new Holy Roman Emperor (who received the Austrian part of the inheritance) and his only son, Philip, who got the rest: Spain, the Italian territories, the Low Countries, and the Spanish territories in the New World, becoming Philip II of Spain.

THE TURKISH ADVANCE

Under Selim I 'the Grim' (r.1512–20) the Turks focused on Persia (Iran) and Egypt, defeating both and, in conquering Egypt, ending a geopolitical division that had lasted over half a millennium.

Under Selim's son, Suleiman the Magnificent (r.1520–66), there were major advances in south-eastern Europe and the Mediterranean. In the former, Belgrade fell in 1521 and Vienna was besieged in 1529. Suleiman did not capture it, but there was no doubt of the direction of travel. In

Hungary, Suleiman initially preferred to exert his influence through its anti-Habsburg ruler János Szapolyai, but after he died in 1540 Suleiman fought directly with the Holy Roman Emperor Charles V's brother Ferdinand, capturing Buda in 1541, Esztergom in 1543, and Temesvár in 1552. In the Mediterranean the Turks captured Rhodes (1522), failed at Malta (1565), and conquered Cyprus (1570–1). Their establishment of a presence in Algiers from 1519 expanded the pressure they could bring to bear into the western Mediterranean.

Even so, in the 16th century Christian-ruled Europe essentially contained external attack, albeit with the loss of much territory, following on from the significant losses suffered since 1356, when the Turks first advanced into Europe.

THE REFORMATION

At the start of the 16th century the Catholic Church sought to be a universal church with standardized practices. There were local variations, not least attachment to particular saints and shrines, and the local recruitment of clerics. However, obedience to the Papacy in Rome remained paramount. Although there were clerical abuses that led to pressure for change, popular devotion to existing religious practices was undeniable.

This situation was to be transformed by the Reformation. There was a pre-history, notably in terms of Lollards in England and Hussites in Bohemia. In 1420–31 the heretical Hussite movement defeated a series of crusades authorized by the Papacy, in part by creating an effective infantry army able to see off heavy cavalry.

The Reformation itself started at Wittenberg in Germany in 1517 when Martin Luther, a priest, attacked the corruption of the Catholic Church. Mishandled by the Church and exploited by princes keen to seize its territories, the Reformation was radicalized. Instead of becoming a revival tendency, the Reformation instead became a new form of Christianity called Protestantism. In turn, that divided, especially into Lutheranism and Calvinism, the latter named after John Calvin, who led the Reformation in Geneva. There was also a radical fringe in the form of the Anabaptists.

Reformation and Counter-Reformation

1420–31	*Hussite Rebellion*
1492	*Jews expelled from Spain*
1517	*Luther posts the 95 Theses*
1521	*Diet of Worms*
1522	*Anabaptism develops as an offshoot of Ulrich Zwingli's reforms*
1529	*Luther and Zwingli meet but are unable to find common ground*
1534	*The Act of Supremacy is passed, confirming England's break from the Roman Church*
1534	*The Society of Jesus is founded*
1536	*John Calvin publishes the* Institutio Christianae Religionis
1536	*Henry VII dissolves the monasteries*
1545–63	*Council of Trent*
1553	*Queen Mary I restores Catholicism to England*
1555	*Peace of Augsburg*
1558	*Queen Elizabeth I returns England to Protestantism*
1559	*John Knox establishes a Protestant Church in Scotland, following the principles of John Calvin*
1562–98	*French Wars of Religion*
1598	*Edict of Nantes grants toleration to Huguenots*

Rejecting the authority of the pope, Protestants sought validation directly from the Bible rather than from the Church. This led them to emphasize the importance of people being able to read the Bible, and they favoured both its publication and its translation into the vernacular (native language) rather than Latin. Literacy therefore became more important. Printing was very significant to the success of the Reformation, as printers were able to produce copies of Luther's sermons more speedily than the Church could destroy them.

The visual panoply of the miraculous world was attacked by the Protestants. In contrast, in the Catholic Counter-Reformation there was an emphasis on 'living saints', including visionaries, stigmatics, mystics, miracle-workers, curers and exorcists, and on art characterized by theatrical effects, notably that of the Baroque.

Protestants found that it was easier to destroy or change the institutions and public practices of medieval Catholicism – to expunge much of its artistic medium, such as stained glass and wall paintings in churches, to prevent pilgrimages, or to abolish monasteries – than to create a new and stable national ecclesiastical order or a national enthusiasm for Protestantism. Illiteracy, which prevented the reading of the translations of the Bible, a shortage of qualified Protestant preachers, and a reluctance to abandon the 'old religion' all limited the spread of Protestantism. However, support from rulers, for example kings in Denmark, Sweden, England and, eventually, Scotland, various princes in the Holy Roman Empire, and the councils of free cities, all ensured the adoption of the Reformation.

Protestantism became the dominant religion in northern Europe including England, where the result of Henry VIII's break with Rome in the 1530s was taken in a more radical direction under Edward VI (r.1547–53). Under Mary (r.1553–8) there was a Catholic reaction, before a moderate Protestantism was established under Elizabeth I (r.1558–1603). Scotland, Geneva, the Netherlands, and parts of Germany followed Calvinist ideas, such as the lack of bishops. Lutheranism was followed in Scandinavia and northern Germany.

A result of the Reformation was division and civil strife, a political world of conspiracy, the search for assistance from foreign co-religionists, and regional, social and factional differences exacerbated by confessional antagonism. Religion provided a spur for the development of resistance theories and practices. This was hardly surprising in a political world in which everything was seen to be at stake because of the prospect of state-directed religious change. States and rulers began to define themselves by their distinctive religious arrangements. This meant, for example, that Catholics could be presented as supporters of hostile foreign powers, making those powers appear even more threatening precisely because of their apparent support at home.

Hans Holbein the Younger's portrait of Henry VIII, painted in 1537. Henry VIII broke with the Catholic faith during the 1530s, following a similar path to many rulers in northern Europe.

THE COUNTER-REFORMATION

The Counter-Reformation was a reform movement directed both against Protestantism and towards a revival of Catholicism. It was launched in Trent, the capital of a prince-bishopric (a territory under the control of a Catholic cleric) in northern Italy, where a Church council opened in 1545 and lasted until 1563. The positive aspects of the Counter-Reformation included the Church's increased and crucial role in social care. However, far less positively, attempts to restore Church unity through doctrinal compromise with Protestantism along with reforms to the Catholic Church were pushed aside in favour of existing Catholic teaching, and a rigid and intolerant approach was taken by the Papacy. An index (list) of forbidden books was drawn up, while the Inquisition became more powerful.

The Counter-Reformation drew on pre-Reformation roots in its efforts to introduce reforms among the clergy, to increase the piety of the laity, in the proselytism of non-believers that was energized by the foundation of the Order of Jesus (the Jesuits), and in the drive to ensure orthodoxy among Christians. This drive to orthodoxy meant that those with different views were treated harshly.

In general, the *autos-da-fé* (burnings) organized by the Inquisition were popular, because those punished as secret Jews or Muslims were mostly outsiders.

The Treatment of Heresy

In Spain, Lucrecia de León, a young woman of modest background born in 1568, was a prophetic dreamer who was seen by her supporters as a divinely-inspired seer. Her dreams criticized the government of Philip II of Spain. In three dreams in 1588 she saw a seven-headed dragon, with the seven deadly sins breathing fire across Spain. Philip ordered the Inquisition to arrest her on charges of heresy and sedition and she was tortured and confined in a convent.

The Council of Trent in 1545 attempted to redress the abuses of medieval Catholicism while condemning Protestantism in no uncertain terms as heresy.

Hostility to Jews and Muslims was longstanding, but was taken forward in the 16th century. In Spain in 1492 and Portugal in 1496 the Jews were ordered to convert to Christianity or to leave. Synagogues were converted into churches. Muslims in Spain in the early 16th century were treated similarly. However, conversion was no longer enough in these paranoid societies. 'Purity-of-blood' laws were passed in order to ban Jewish *conversos* from particular honours and positions, while the *Moriscos* (converted Muslims) were expelled from Spain in 1609. This purging of society reflected the imposition of the ideological norm of authoritarian Catholicism.

In the Counter-Reformation, particularly between 1580 and 1648, Protestantism was defeated in what became Belgium, France, Austria, the Czech Republic, Hungary, Slovakia, Poland and much of Germany. The French Wars of Religion ended in 1598 and then resumed, leading to a Catholic victory in 1629. The Valois dynasty came to an end with the assassination of Henry III in 1589 while besieging Paris. The Protestant leader, Henry of Navarre, converted to Catholicism in order to be crowned King Henry IV of France in 1594.

The Dutch Revolt (1568–1609 and 1621–48) and the Thirty Years' War (1618–48) ended with both the Low Countries and Germany divided between Protestantism and Catholicism. Catholic rulers were driven from Scotland and Sweden, and Catholic Ireland was conquered by England.

The French Wars of Religion, 1562–98

Alongside religious division and political failure in France, the breakdown of the political and governmental system meant resources could not be consolidated behind a large army, resulting in military collapse. Foreign intervention in France, particularly by Spain on behalf of the French Catholics and by England on that of the rival Protestant Huguenots, complicated the situation. Compromise ended the wars in 1598. Henry IV (Henry of Navarre) had converted to Catholicism in 1593 in order to gain control of Paris (supposedly saying that 'Paris is worth a mass'). He had to compromise with the Catholic League, Spain and, via the Edict of Nantes, with the Huguenots, who gained the right to fortify towns. This right reflected the power they already wielded.

THE AGE OF SPAIN

There was nothing on the global scale to match Spain's imperial success. Spain was better able than its enemies to sustain the challenge of large scale and protracted warfare because Spain had the advantages of New World silver, credit facilities based in part on this silver, and the capacity to mobilize resources across its empire. In the 1560s Spain focused on conflict with the Turks, a process that culminated in the battle of Lepanto in 1571, a large-scale galley engagement in which the Turks were beaten, and in a subsequent struggle for control over Tunis.

The Escorial

El Escorial, *the royal palace and monastery near Madrid, was built in 1563–84 to the order of Philip II and was designed as a declaration of Spain's role as the defender of Christendom. There have been a number of explanations of the gridiron floor plan; for example, that it honoured St Lawrence, who was roasted to death on a grill, or that it was based on descriptions of the Temple of Solomon, who was a figure of great interest to Philip.*

In the mid-1570s Spain turned instead to playing the leading role in the Wars of Religion (1562–98) within Western Europe. Spanish successes demonstrated its unmatched power in Christian Europe: the conquest of Portugal in 1580; the reconquest in the 1580s of much of the Low Countries, where Philip was faced by the Dutch Revolt; the initially successful intervention in the French Wars of Religion; the ability to thwart the English attacks on Portugal and the Spanish New World; and continuing dominance of Italy. However, the attempt by the Spanish Armada to invade England in 1588 failed totally, while in the 1590s Philip II could not reconquer the northern Netherlands or prevent his allies losing in France.

The Dutch Revolt

The highly unpopular religious and fiscal policies of the ruler, Philip II of Spain, and his neglect of the Dutch nobility, led, in 1566-7, to a breakdown of control. In 1566, the Calvinists seized churches and destroyed their Catholic images, a dramatic break with the past.

---

*Concerned about his duty to the church and about the danger that
the crisis might benefit Protestantism and French goals, Philip sent a
large army under a veteran general, Ferdinand, 3rd Duke of Alba,
to restore order. Arriving in 1567, Alba imposed unpopular new
taxes and treated opponents harshly. However, this encouraged fresh
opposition from 1572. Alba's brutality failed to suppress opposition.
However, major divisions between Catholics and Protestants among
the rebels and the developing radicalism of the Protestant cities of
Brabant, notably Bruges and Ghent, led to a collapse of the revolt's
precarious unity, particularly from 1577. The Catholic nobles of
the south proved willing to reconcile themselves with Philip and
to restore social discipline. Combined with successful Spanish
campaigning in the south in the 1580s this was the basis of what
became two states: Catholic Belgium, which remained under
Spanish control, and the independent Protestant Netherlands.*

*Religious antagonism made it impossible for Philip II, with his
rigid Catholicism, to compromise and also undermined the practice of
political incorporation. As a result, Philip had far less success with the
Dutch Revolt than with opposition in Italy, Portugal and Aragon.*

THE SPANISH ARMADA

The armada was part of an attempt to overcome Queen Elizabeth I of
England, and thus end English support for the Dutch cause, and involved
a fleet proceeding up the English Channel in order to cover an invasion of
England by Spanish troops in Belgium. It was based on flawed planning
about the nature of joint operations and did not succeed. The Spanish
fleet fought its way along the English Channel, retaining its cohesion and
strength in the face of persistent English attacks. But before it could drive
off the English and Dutch ships blockading the Spanish invasion barges
in Belgian ports, the Spanish fleet was disrupted by English attack and
driven off into the North Sea. It then sought to sail back to Spain around
Scotland and Ireland, but was badly pummelled by storms in the process.

The Spanish Armada sent in 1588 to invade England presented a formidable force. English and Dutch ships were able to damage the Spanish fleet enough to force it to return to Spain.

THE CRISIS OF SPAIN

Historians have often employed the image of Don Quixote tilting at a windmill in the novel by Cervantes to represent an unrealistic Spain foolishly taking on too much in its quest for glory. The famous and instructive metaphor serves as a widespread narrative of Spanish decline, if not collapse. The great world empire of 1598 suffered defeats by France, England and the Dutch over the following century. In addition, there were serious economic difficulties in the 17th century, possibly due to global cooling. Philip IV of Spain (r.1621–65) also faced rebellions, notably in Portugal and Catalonia in 1640, as part of what many historians call a 'mid-17th century crisis' also seen in the British Isles, France, the Netherlands and Russia. The first rebellion against Philip, in a war that lasted until 1668, eventually left Portugal independent, while Catalonia was only reconquered after major efforts.

Despite its supposed 'decline,' Spain actually enjoyed considerable success in the first three decades of the 17th century. However, it could not sustain this situation. Continuous conflict from 1621 until 1668 put terrible pressure on its finances, but also on administrative and political structures and systems. The fiscal burdens of war posed growing political problems. The attempt in 1624 to introduce a Union of Arms, in which regions of Spain raised troops in relation to their population and size, was rejected by Catalonia and in 1627 the government went bankrupt. A crisis caused by the burdens of war support and by attempts to share the cost sparked the Catalan rising in 1640. There was another successful rebellion in Portugal that year, and unsuccessful risings in Naples and Sicily.

THE BRITISH ISLES IN THE 16TH CENTURY

The Reformation became closely involved in relations between England, Scotland and Wales. Scottish independence from England was linked to Scotland's alliance with France, which repeatedly led to conflict, with the Scottish king James IV killed during defeat at Flodden in 1512. France's championing of the Catholic cause and the progress of the Reformation in Scotland caused the overthrow of Mary Queen of Scots, and she was replaced by her young Protestant son, James VI. The acceptance of the Reformation by Scotland and Wales was crucial to their integration into a British consciousness and policy. However, Ireland rejected the Reformation, and this encouraged its conquest by the English as claims to rule by the English Crown were enforced.

In many ways the British Isles appeared distinct from the rest of Europe. The Church of England, the size and importance of London, the role of the Common Law, the small size of the army, were in some ways unique to the island state. The Common Law tradition (based on case law and precedent rather than a codified set of laws) was significant for legal, intellectual and political divergence between Britain and continental Europe, where codified Roman Law prevailed. For example, the English jury system ensured popular participation in justice. London promoted the interaction of bourgeois and aristocratic thinking and values, and the influence of commercial considerations upon national policy.

Elizabeth I (r.1558–1603) was the longest-reigning monarch since Edward III (r.1312–1377). This longevity provided an opportunity for the consolidation of the Elizabethan Church settlement, the development of a measure of political stability, and the establishment of a generally acceptable Protestant succession. Her reign saw England's commercial expansion, the state's financial development, the growth of the city of London and the flowering of drama. The benefits of this lengthy lifespan contrasts with France, where a series of short reigns was linked to the assassinations of Henry III in 1589 and Henry IV in 1610.

The Rise Of Opera

Opera was a particularly striking and new art form and its development reflected the energy and flexibility of European culture, and the role of both court and public patronage. Claudio Monteverdi (1567–1643) was employed by the Duke of Mantua from 1602 to 1612, and during that time he developed a new type of entertainment, opera, with Orfeo *(1607) and* Arianna *(1608). There had been significant precursors, such as interludes between the acts of plays, and verse dramas accompanied by music. But Monteverdi produced a musical unity, drafting his music on a large scale. Mantua, Ferrara, Florence and Venice all became significant centres of musical innovation.*

THE CRISIS OF BRITAIN

Created in 1603, the personal union between Scotland and England, which James VI of Scotland and James I of England termed Great Britain, broke down as a result of the policies of Charles I (r.1625–49). Lacking common sense, flexibility and pragmatism, Charles was devious and untrustworthy. His belief in order and in the dignity of kingship led him to take an unsympathetic and arrogant attitude to any disagreement. Tension over his extraordinary financial demands and apparently crypto-Catholic ecclesiastical policies sapped support for Charles in England, but the breakdown actually occurred in Scotland, leading to the Bishops' Wars (1639–40). This marked the start of the Civil Wars and was symptomatic of the whole period of conflict. Charles mishandled the situation and lost, religion played a major role in the war, and it involved different parts of the British Isles, each of which were divided.

The crisis forced Charles to turn to Parliament in England, but the period of his 'personal rule' without Parliament since 1629 had generated grievances and much fear about his intentions. In an atmosphere of mounting crisis, the need to raise an army to deal with a major Catholic rising in Ireland in November 1641 polarized the situation. Debate over who was to control this army exacerbated tensions over parliamentary pressure for a change in Church government. The power and authority of both Crown and Parliament came to the fore and were in conspicuous opposition to each other.

Fighting in England started in July 1642. Repeated successes led to Parliamentary victory in 1646. This victory was due in part to the support of the wealthiest regions of England and Scotland, and to the folly of Charles; fighting ability, command skills and chance also played major roles.

Having won, the victors fell out. In 1648 the Scots invaded England on behalf of Charles, only to be defeated. The army under Oliver Cromwell followed up its victory by purging Parliament. Charles was tried and executed for treason in 1649 and England was declared a republic.

Cromwell pressed on to conquer Ireland and then Scotland, before seizing power in 1653. This was a military regime shot through with an intolerant sense of divine purpose. Cromwell died in 1658, and the weak and divided republican regime was overthrown in 1660, leading to a restored monarchy in the shape of Charles II.

THE SECOND SERFDOM

The transformation of rural society in Eastern Europe towards a 'second serfdom,' with heavy labour services performed by the peasantry, was a response to the demand for grain exports to other parts of Europe, especially rising demand in Western Europe following rapid population growth in the 16th century (after limited growth in the 15th century). This demand was met in particular by rye exports from Poland via the major rivers, notably the Vistula and the Niemen. This export made control over the relevant ports, such as Danzig (Gdansk) for the Vistula, crucially important. This was also true of the 'Sound' between the Baltic and the North Sea. Thanks to the export of grain, iron and timber from the Baltic, it played a greater role in European history than at any stage since the Viking age. Moreover, trade through the Baltic joined Eastern and Western Europe, and financed a specialization in each that sustained the 'Second Serfdom.'

The Second Serfdom itself had a longer genesis. It was preceded by 15th-century changes, as lords who had gained private possession of public jurisdictions responded to the economic problems of the late medieval period, particularly lower demand and fixed cash incomes. The Second Serfdom held back the spread of the money economy in Eastern Europe as it ensured the continual provision of food or services, and not money, for transactions such as rent.

War and Money

Wars had to be fought by borrowing, which required the ability to call on domestic and international credit networks. The Habsburgs called on the Fugger banking family of Augsburg and on the merchant financiers of Genoa. France called on bankers in Lyons and Venice. Dutch and English public finance came to be focused on institutions; the Bank of Amsterdam and the Bank of England were founded in 1650 and 1694 respectively.

THE STRUGGLE FOR THE BALTIC

The Baltic region was the major source of European shipbuilding materials and an exporter of grain, copper and iron. It became unstable in the 16th century for a number of reasons. In 1523 the Union of Kalmar, which had bound Denmark, Norway, Sweden and Finland together under one crown from 1397, finally collapsed. In its place two opposing states, Denmark (which also ruled Norway) and Sweden (which also ruled Finland), came to compete for hegemony in the north.

Meanwhile, the expansion of Russian power towards the Baltic threatened the political stability of the lands on its eastern shores. Novgorod fell to the Russians in 1477 and Pskov in 1510, and Lithuania was attacked in 1500–3, 1507–8 and 1512–15, leading to the capture of Smolensk in 1514.

In addition, the Reformation raised a question over what would happen to the extensive lands of the crusading orders such as the Teutonic Knights and the Livonian Order. The Reformation also separated Catholic Poland from Protestant Denmark and Sweden. (Despite both being Lutheran, Denmark and Sweden were also bitter rivals.) Meanwhile, Ivan IV, or 'the Terrible', of Russia (r.1533–84) found Denmark and Sweden to be his firm opponents, while Poland, Lithuania and Ukraine, which formed a union in 1569, opposed his attempt to advance to the Baltic.

Further west, war between Denmark and Sweden was linked to the establishment of the new Vasa dynasty on the throne of Sweden and, in the 1520s and 1530s, to conflict between Protestants and Catholics. Religious rivalry became a far more potent theme in war between Sweden and Poland, a conflict sharpened by rivalry from the 1590s between the different branches of the Vasa family that ruled in each state. The Poles did well in exploiting Russian disunity during the 'Time of Troubles' (1604–13), but were finally driven from Russia. In the 1620s Gustav Adolf of Sweden (r.1611–32) conquered Livonia from the Poles, although he found them difficult opponents.

THE RISE OF RUSSIA

The rise of Russia was a steady development in Eastern Europe, which was only interrupted by the division and foreign invasions of the 'Time of Troubles' (1604–13). Under Ivan IV (r.1533–84) the longstanding struggle with Islam resulted in two important successes for Russia. The first, after much effort from 1545, was the capture in 1552 of Kazan, the most northerly Islamic state. After Kazan fell to Ivan IV there were serious insurgencies (1553–6) but these were repressed with great brutality, which reflected longstanding fear and anger based on conflict with and slave-raiding by Kazan, and religious hostility toward Muslims.

Ivan the Terrible helped to transform Russia from a limited medieval state into a vast empire, but he faced significant opposition from his western neighbours.

The conquest of Kazan opened the way for expansion down the Volga to Astrakhan, which the Russians conquered in 1556, then towards the Caucasus and across the Urals into western Siberia. This success was highly significant for the reconfiguration of the geopolitics of Eurasia, both in the short and the long term.

This was no easy process. Invasions of central Muscovy by the Crimean Tatars brought serious devastation in the 16th century. Moscow was sacked in 1571 and much of its population taken away as slaves.

THE THIRTY YEARS' WAR

The Thirty Years' War (1618–48) was effectively a Europe-wide civil war which brought together several different conflicts: an Austrian Habsburg attempt to assert authority in the Empire; hostilities in the long war between Spain and the Dutch; rivalry between France and Spain; and a dynastic struggle within the Vasa family between the rulers of Poland and Sweden.

The war initially began as a rising in 1618 against Habsburg authority in Bohemia (modern Czech Republic). This rising fused Bohemian antipathy to the terms of Habsburg control, Protestant opposition to a Catholic zeal that was becoming more threatening as the Counter-Reformation gathered pace, and the strength of aristocratic politics. A Protestant ruler, Frederick, Elector of the Palatinate, was elected by rebel Bohemian nobles. This rising was crushed by superior forces at the Battle of the White Mountain outside Prague (1620). Habsburg authority was then reimposed and Bohemia was re-Catholicized. This was accompanied by the expropriation of the estates of aristocrats who had rebelled and the creation of a new aristocracy from the supporters of Holy Roman Emperor Ferdinand II.

After the Bohemians offered the throne to Frederick, in 1620 Spanish and Bavarian forces overran his Palatinate. War resumed between the Dutch and Spain in 1621, after a 12-year truce negotiated in 1609 came to an end, and the Dutch then encouraged opposition to the Habsburgs in Germany. Emperor Ferdinand II entrusted his troops to a Bohemian military entrepreneur, Albrecht von Wallenstein, who won a series of victories, as did Tilly, the Bavarian general of the Catholic

League. Christian IV of Denmark intervened in Germany in 1625 on the Protestant side, only to be defeated in 1626. Denmark itself was invaded and forced out of the war in 1629. Habsburg power now reached to the Baltic and Spain, Austria and Poland were all aligned.

Ferdinand dominated the Empire until the Swedish invasion of 1630, but he failed to use this period to win support and consolidate his position. In addition, French mediation rescued King Gustav Adolf of Sweden (r.1611–32) from an indecisive war with Poland in 1629 and in 1630 he landed in Germany. He advanced south, crushing Tilly at Breitenfeld (1631), which led many German Protestant princes to rally to Sweden. Gustav then advanced into central Germany, going on to invade Bavaria in 1632. Later that year Wallenstein and Gustav fought at Lützen in Saxony, a fog-shrouded and largely inconclusive battle, in which both sides lost about one-third of their strength and Gustav was killed.

In 1634 the increasingly independent Wallenstein was killed by some

In the Battle of Nördlingen of 1634, a Catholic alliance of Austrian and Spanish troops inflicted a significant defeat over the smaller Protestant Swedish army: the Swedes were outnumbered 33,000 to 25,000. Nördlingen was followed by a retreat of Swedish power in Germany.

of his own officers on the orders of the Emperor, and in the same year at Nördlingen an Austro-Spanish army heavily defeated the Swedes, driving them from southern Germany. This led in 1635 to France's entry into the war to resist Habsburg hegemony. The war went back and forth over the following years, but by the late 1640s the Habsburgs were under great pressure from Swedish forces in Bohemia and French ones in southern Germany.

In 1648 the Peace of Westphalia ended the war. It left the Habsburgs dominant in their hereditary lands (principally Austria and Bohemia) until their empire collapsed in 1918. In contrast, the German princes were left in greater control of their own territories. France gained control over much of Alsace, while Brandenburg-Prussia gained much territory and emerged ahead of Saxony as the leading north German Protestant state, and the Swedes gained control over the estuaries of the Elbe, Oder and Weser. Sweden had passed Denmark in the power stakes, a process underlined in conflict between the two in the late 1650s.

The Westphalia settlement served as the basis for European international relations until the French Revolution. It provided a framework both for politics within Germany and for the more general practice of diplomacy. At the same time, the settlement did not cover Eastern Europe which was where international relations were to change most over the following century. Moreover, in Western Europe the settlement was only maintained as a result of war.

CHAPTER 6
FROM THE BAROQUE
TO NAPOLEON
1650–1815

The 'long 18th century,' that from the mid-17th century crisis to the fall of Napoleon in 1815, was a period of turmoil, with international conflict matched by political uncertainty. Most of the economy remained based on agriculture, with society dominated by the landed aristocracy. At the same time, there were significant centres of urban life and Atlantic Europe was of growing commercial importance.

THE SIEGE OF VIENNA, 1683

The siege of Vienna was a remarkably dramatic confrontation. Rather than focusing on border forts, the Turks, under Kara Mustafa, Grand Vizier of the Ottoman Empire (r.1676–83), marched directly on Vienna, which they surrounded on 16 July. The Turks used both bombardment and mines to weaken the defences. The garrison suffered heavy casualties in its defence, as well as losses from dysentery. The Turks, who were poorly prepared to lay siege to such a powerful position with its deep moat and large ramparts, suffered similarly. Nevertheless, during August the city's outer defences steadily succumbed. The Turks lacked heavy-calibre cannon and were outgunned so they relied on undermining the defences, which they did with some success, leading to breaches where there was then bitter fighting. On 4 September the garrison fired distress rockets to urge the assembling relief force to attack the Turkish forces. On 12 September it did so and routed the Turkish army. Victorious, the Austrians then advanced to conquer Hungary, capturing Buda in 1686 after they had failed two years earlier.

On 12 September 1683 the forces of the Holy Roman Empire successfully routed the Ottoman army outside Vienna, ending the Turkish advance into Europe.

THE RISE OF ABSOLUTISM

Reacting to the disorder and instability of the 16th and early 17th centuries, rulers across Europe sought to strengthen their position during this period, resulting in a governmental system known as 'absolutism'. Traditionally seen in terms of powerful governments, this later came to represent the concept of co-operation between the Crown and the aristocracy. Clear hostility to the idea of despotism and conventions of acceptable royal behaviour limited the possibilities for royal action. The monarchy was expected to operate within a context of legality and tradition, and this made new initiatives hazardous politically and difficult administratively.

The Culture of The Baroque

The prime cultural style of the late 17th and early 18th centuries, the Baroque was particularly prominent in the Catholic centres of Italy and Spain, but was also found elsewhere, including in Protestant Europe. The style, which emphasized symmetry and coherence, could be seen in architecture (with the work of Bernini and Wren), music (Bach), drama (Dryden), and other creative forms. Sacral monarchy was important to the Baroque. St Paul's Cathedral remains an affirmation of religious values by means of Baroque magnificence.

This period saw an emphasis on uniformity within states, which caused problems for religious minorities; for example, the legal status of the Huguenots (French Protestants), which had been secured by the Edict of Nantes of 1598, was revoked by another royal edict in 1685. Tolerance was regarded as a sign of weakness and failure by such rulers.

Governments focused their domestic policies on avoiding disorder and on raising funds for war. Royal histories encouraged this attitude by lauding the winning of glory through war, previous royal 'heroes', and noted how dynasties had established themselves through conflict (including the Bourbons in France, Spain and Naples, the Tudors in England and the Romanovs in Russia).

Louis XIV deliberately displayed his majesty as 'The Sun King' in his spectacular new palace at Versailles, setting a pattern that would also be seen elsewhere, as in Berlin, Stockholm, and Het Loo in the Netherlands, the palace of Louis' most persistent opponent, William III of Orange. These palaces provided impressive backdrops for a theatrical account of royal power, which clearly distinguished the monarch as a special figure.

A very different demonstration of power was provided by the many fortresses built for Louis XIV by Sébastien Le Prestre de Vauban. Appointed commissioner general of fortifications in 1678, he supervised the construction of 33 new fortresses and the renovation of many more.

Some rulers sought to copy Louis, but others saw him as a dangerous warning. Concerns that James II (r.1685–8) was taking England in an absolutist direction led to conspiracy in 1688. A Catholic, James was ruling without Parliament (as his father had done from 1629 to 1640) and increasing the size of the army. The rebellion succeeded because it was supported by an invasion by William III of Orange, the key figure

*Louis XIV was the pinnacle of absolutist monarchy who displayed his power through building an
impressive royal palace at Versailles.*

in Dutch politics, who was also James' nephew and son-in-law. James
proved unable to deal with the crisis and fled.

Having seized power, William had himself and his wife Mary declared
joint sovereigns. A new constitutional and political system was introduced
and the events were later described as the 'Glorious Revolution'. The
crucial element was parliamentary power, in total contrast to France
where the Estates General did not meet once between 1648 and 1789.

Similarly, the *Cortes* in Portugal did not meet in the 18th century. In England, Parliament met annually and there were regular elections, and the Triennial Act of 1694 made government finances dependent on parliamentary support.

As a result there were very different constitutional models for strong states available to Europe from the late 17th century. The United Provinces (the Dutch Republic) was a strong state and a republic. In contrast, England offered a monarchical alternative to France. William III's successful invasion ensured that the Westminster Parliament diverged from the more general tendency towards a smaller, or even non-existent, role for representative institutions.

THE RUSSIAN EMPIRE

At the start of the 17th century, during the 'Time of Troubles' and soon after the end of the reign of Ivan the Terrible, Russia came close to collapse. Alongside serious rebellion and social disorder, foreign invasion by both Poles and Swedes culminated in a Polish garrison in Moscow. This provided the background for a new dynasty, the Romanovs, who defeated foreign enemies and strengthened Russia domestically. Tsar Michael founded the dynasty in 1613. His son Tsar Alexis (r.1645–76) was a key figure who established Russian power in Ukraine, but was also somewhat traditional in his image of Russian monarchy, including its link with the Orthodox Church.

Nevertheless, Russia was not overthrown and, from the 1680s, the Russians made major efforts to project their strength south across the steppe in order to crush the Tatars. Unsuccessful in the 1680s, the Russians were victorious in 1696, when Azov fell, again from 1736 to 1739, in the 1768–74 war, and finally in 1783, when Crimea was annexed. During their drive southwards the Russians relied heavily on building lines of outposts that were intended both to contain the Tatars and to bring the Cossacks under control. A line was built at the beginning of the 17th century between the rivers Don and Vorskla and was followed by other lines successively further south. The spread of a system of local government supervised by the Moscow Military Chancellery greatly eased the necessary mobilization of resources for the move south.

Peter the Great as painted by Maria Clementi (1692–1761). Peter I prided himself on his military prowess and often personally led his armies into battle.

In contrast, his son Peter, later 'Peter the Great,' took a new approach to rule. Peter had a Western European upbringing. Born in 1672, he became joint-Tsar with his half-brother Ivan V in 1682, while an older half-sister, Sophia, acted as regent. In 1689, Peter overthrew Sophia, while Ivan died in 1696 and Peter became sole ruler. On his journey to England and the Dutch Republic in 1697–8, he witnessed a model of progress that he sought to emulate and implement. In 1712 he moved the capital from Moscow to St Petersburg, the new city he founded on the Baltic in 1703, having taken the site from the Swedes. This was both a practical and a highly symbolic act. St Petersburg's position was more outward looking than Moscow's, and Peter was able to control the layout of the new city.

Russia from Principality to Empire

1547	*Ivan IV 'the Terrible' is crowned as Tsar of all the Russias*
1552	*Siege of Kazan*
1556	*Annexation of Astrakhan*
1570–2	*Russo-Crimean Wars*
1571	*Sack of Moscow*
1580	*Russian Cossacks invade Siberia*
1598–1613	*The Time of Troubles*
1605–18	*Polish–Muscovite War*
1613	*Tsar Michael founds the Romanov Dynasty*
1632–4	*Smolensk War*
1689	*Peter the Great becomes Tsar*
1696	*Conquest of Azov*
1700–21	*Great Northern War*
1709	*Battle of Poltava*
1712	*St Petersburg is made Russia's capital*
1773–5	*Pugachev Rising*
1783	*Annexation of Crimea*

Peter also sought to make the nobility act as servants of modernization and organized them in a Table of Ranks. The role of the Orthodox Church was reduced, and a series of ministries, as well as a fleet, were created. Although major governmental, ecclesiastical, military and economic reforms were pushed through, many were only partially implemented. Peter helped to give Russian government and élite society a western orientation which widened the gulf between it and the bulk of the population. He impressed many foreign commentators, including the French philosopher and writer Voltaire, but was unpopular in Russia, where he was widely regarded as a diabolical changeling.

Peter spent much of his reign at war, notably with Sweden in the Great Northern War (1700–21), but also with the Turks (1689–98, but begun earlier by his predecessor, then again in 1710–11). Peter also invaded Persia (1722–3). Acting as a modern war leader, Peter led his army to the sieges of Azov in 1695 and 1696, on the Pruth expedition in 1711, and on the advance into Persia in 1722. He won particular success at the battle of Poltava (1709), defeating an invasion led by Charles XII of Sweden. Peter went on to conquer modern-day Estonia and much of modern-day Latvia, both of which were annexed in the Peace of Nystad in 1721, although Finland, another gain, was returned to Sweden.

His successors, particularly his widow Catherine I (r.1725–7), consolidated his position and, with the exception of Peter II (r.1727–30), they continued Peter's policy of Westernization. None of them enjoyed Peter's fame, until Catherine the Great (Catherine II, r.1762–96), but they were all part of a process in which Russia was increasingly part of the European system. Indeed, Russian troops moved west into Germany in 1735 and 1748 and briefly occupied Berlin in 1760.

The Pugachev Rising, 1773–5
The largest-scale insurgency of the 18th century was launched by Cossacks from the Urals region under Yemelyan Pugachev, who claimed to be the dead Tsar Peter III of the Russian Empire. Its numbers were swelled with peasant runaways, especially from the

harsh working conditions of the mines and metallurgical plants of the Ural Mountains. Regular farming serfs also played a major role. Some disgruntled priests, some townspeople, and some unhappy members of the lower service echelons of the nobility joined in. Having captured the major city of Kazan in 1774, killing those in Western dress, Pugachev promised freedom to the serfs, which led to the widespread slaughter of the nobility. However, disorganization and divisions among the rebels, and the army's greater ability to focus on the rebellion after peace was negotiated with the Turks in 1774, led to Pugachev's failure. He was executed with great cruelty, reflecting the fear his insurgency had generated.

SCIENTIFIC DEVELOPMENT

Important advances in physics were followed later in the 18th century by others in chemistry, notably the discovery of new gaseous elements. The application of new concepts proved difficult, but developments in physics lay behind James Watt's significant improvement of the steam engine. There were other bases for improvement. The combination of glassmaking and the use of glasses helped in the standardization of both equipment and measurement. Moreover, better eyesight as a result of spectacles encouraged an emphasis on realism and helped retain the skills of the elderly.

Newton and the Rise of Science
The British scientist Sir Isaac Newton (1642–1727) was one of the most important and influential scientists in history, being responsible for key developments in astronomy, mathematics and physics. He published the Mathematical Principles of Natural Philosophy *in 1687, outlining a new understanding of universal mechanics and gravitation that rested on an idea of a unity of Earth and Heavens, the latter open to scrutiny by telescopes and affected by the same*

> *physical laws. Newton discovered calculus, universal gravitation and formulated the laws of motion. President of the Royal Society from 1703 to 1727, he helped make science truly prestigious, both in Britain and on the continent.*

EUROPE AND THE WORLD ECONOMY

The unique European experience of creating a global network of empire and trade across the oceans was based on a distinctive interaction between economy, technology and state formation. This process ushered in a new period of world history.

Economic gains encouraged the projection of European maritime power, while applied science fostered maritime development. Rulers and ministers eagerly supported trans-oceanic trade in an attempt to benefit from the developing global market economy. However, competition between European powers had an adverse effect, especially on Portugal in the 17th century.

Ironically Europe was sometimes adversely affected by imports from further afield. From the 16th century, silver from the Americas had contributed to inflation and in the 17th century, plantation goods, notably sugar and tobacco, had a growing impact on Europeans' diet and pastimes. Indeed, the world economy changed the nature of European addiction, with sugar, tobacco, tea and coffee added to the already strong influence of alcohol.

EUROPEAN EMPIRES: COLONIES AND COMPANIES

Colonies became more important to the political and economic calculations of the Atlantic European states during the 18th century. Britain made inroads into the French empire, most notably acquiring Canada under the Peace of Paris of 1763. However, Britain had less success against Spain's empire.

In some parts of the world, especially the Indian Ocean, European imperial activity was organized by trading companies that were permitted to raise forces. (However, this method was less important when there were already large numbers of European settlers.) The Dutch and English East India Companies were emulated by a number of others, including the French, Danish, Austrian and Swedish. The Dutch West Indian Company failed to drive the Portuguese from Brazil from the 1630s to the 1650s, while the English Royal African Company was unable to dominate the slave trade from West Africa, but England's Hudson Bay Company was the key player in the North American fur trade, and was a territorial power in northern Canada.

Emigration was significant in the Atlantic world. European settlers moved there in large numbers, especially from Britain to North America. Far fewer settlers moved to Africa and the Indian Ocean than to the New World. There was also the involuntary migration of slaves from Africa to the New World. They were used to address the labour shortages in the colonies that were caused by the limited size of the original population, which was further gravely hit by disease. About 10.7 million slaves were taken to the New World, the largest number to the Portuguese colony of Brazil. Many others went to British, French and Spanish colonies in the Caribbean. They were principally used as plantation labour, notably in the production of sugar, tobacco, coffee, rice and cotton.

The liberal political systems of the Dutch and Britain, in contrast to those of state-directed systems, were particularly successful in eliciting the co-operation of their own and other countries' capitalists, producing a symbiosis of government and the private sector that proved both effective and valuable, in particular for developing naval strength. Profit encouraged compromise, although this was not without costs and did not encompass everyone. The possibility of profit also acted as a strong stimulus to technological development and improved organization for war, trade and colonization. These factors were to frame the 19th-century world.

THE ENLIGHTENMENT

In the 18th century, the tendency in Europe towards the application of reason became almost a cult. Although it was not a coherent movement, this application, which is known as the Enlightenment, sought to combine utilitarianism (a moral code based on creating the greatest happiness among the greatest number of people) and the search for individual happiness.

In practice, these impulses and their impact were very varied. In Italy and Poland, although there were reforming tendencies, there was not the criticism of Catholicism that was seen in France. The key element of Enlightenment thinking was a belief in the improvability of human arrangements and in the value of applying reason. As a result, there was an overlap between the Enlightenment and the concurrent Scientific Revolution. Leading figures in the Enlightenment movement, which certainly had a celebrity culture, included the French writers Voltaire and Rousseau. The most prominent product was the *Encyclopédie*.

'Enlightened despots' included Frederick II 'the Great' of Prussia (r.1740–86), Catherine II, 'the Great' of Russia (r.1762–96), Joseph II of Austria (r.1780–90) and Gustav III of Sweden (r.1771–92), and ministers such as the Marquis of Pombal, who dominated Portugal from 1755 to 1777. They wanted stronger states, in order to be able to cope with the strains of international competition, and notably to support large armies.

The *Encyclopédie* (Encyclopedia)

The systematization and application of knowledge were themes that illuminated the Encyclopédie, *a major French synthesis of Enlightenment views. Launched by Denis Diderot and Jean le Rond d'Alembert in 1751, originally to translate Ephraim Chambers' attempt to organize and cross-reference knowledge contained in his* Cyclopaedia, *or* An University Dictionary of Arts and Sciences *(1728), it became a work of reference and also a vehicle for propaganda for the ideas of the philosophes. In an article called* 'Encyclopédie', *Diderot wrote that by helping people to become better informed, such a work would help them become more virtuous and happier. As a guide to the known, the* Encyclopédie *was not interested in speculating about the unknown, and this focus encouraged a sense of human achievement, as well as distancing the work from the occult and the mystical. It was also published in the vernacular (native language).*

THE DECLINE OF THE JESUITS

The suppression of the Jesuits represented a decisive break with Counter-Reformation Catholicism. The Jesuits were an international religious order with a special oath of loyalty to the Papacy and while they were envied within the Church, their fall was more a triumph of state over church. Expelled from Portugal in 1759, the order was suppressed in France in 1764 and in Spain and Naples in 1767. Pope Clement XIV was bullied by the Bourbon rulers of France, who seized the papal enclaves of Avignon and Benevento, into abolishing the Jesuit order in 1773. This also reflected the declining prestige of the Papacy. The Jesuit order was then suppressed in the remaining Catholic states. The Jesuits were abolished due to the anger of Catholic courts not of Enlightenment intellectuals.

The Jesuits' educational and pastoral roles were largely taken over by other bodies, but the suppression of the order reflected little credit on those who carried it out. Many of the Jesuits were brutally treated and many useful institutions were destroyed or harmed. Two Hungarian ex-Jesuit poets, Ferenc Faludi and David Szabó, saw the suppression as the death of a culture that was a symptom of the decline of European society. It certainly marked the passing of the 'old' Europe.

THE HOLY ROMAN EMPIRE UNDER THE HABSBURGS

Together with the Papacy, the Holy Roman Empire was the most important constitutional survivor from the Middle Ages. The empire covered roughly the area of modern Germany, Austria and Bohemia, under an elected emperor and with a number of common institutions, such as a 'diet' (assembly) at Ratisbon (Regensburg) and an imperial court at Wetzlar. From 1438 to 1740 and 1745 to 1806, the emperors were always members of the Habsburg family, the rulers of Austria, Bohemia and Christian Hungary. In 1742, in the absence of a male Habsburg, Charles Albert of Bavaria was crowned as Emperor Charles VII.

The power and authority of successive emperors was limited, especially in northern Germany and particularly after the Thirty Years' War, by the strength of the major principalities, including Prussia, Hanover, Saxony and Bavaria. A measure of unity could be obtained in the face of common adversaries, such as the Turks from 1683 to 1699 and Louis XIV of

France from 1702 to 1714. In the late 1710s and early 1720s, Charles VI had had some success in reviving imperial authority. But from the mid-1730s it was weakened by Austro-Prussian animosity. The policies and intentions of Joseph II, Emperor from 1765 to 1790 and ruler of Austria from 1780 to 1790, were widely feared. German unity required a new forum if it was to have much of a future.

In 1806 the Holy Roman Empire was dissolved. The last emperor, Francis II, became Emperor of Austria; while much of Germany joined the Confederation of the Rhine, a body that excluded Austrian influence. These changes were made in response to Napoleon's wishes.

AN ERA OF WAR

Conflict occurred frequently in the late 17th and early 18th centuries, in part because rulers pursued their interests without any effective system of peaceful arbitration. These wars encouraged large-scale investment in armies and navies, which put a strain on domestic politics.

I. Anglo–Dutch Wars

Three wars (1652–4, 1665–7 and 1672–4) saw naval and colonial confrontations between Europe's two leading Protestant naval powers. Control over trade routes proved a key element. By 1674 England had clearly overtaken the Dutch as the leading Protestant power in North America. Once captured, New Amsterdam was renamed New York after the Lord High Admiral, James, Duke of York, who later became King James II.

II. War of The Spanish Succession, 1701–14

This was a wide-ranging struggle for the succession to the inheritance of the Spanish Habsburgs after Charles II of Spain (r.1665–1700) died without children. Louis XIV of France backed his own second son, who became Philip V of Spain (r.1700–46), against the Austrian Archduke Charles, who was backed by Britain and the Dutch. Philip fought off his opponents in Spain, but the French were defeated in what became Belgium, Germany and Italy, notably at the battles of Blenheim (1704) and Turin (1706). As a result of the war, the succession was partitioned.

Charles, who had become the Emperor Charles VI (r.1711–40) on the death of his elder brother, gained Lombardy, Naples, Belgium and Sardinia for Austria, and exchanged Sardinia for Sicily with Victor Amadeus II of Savoy-Piedmont in 1720. Philip gained the rest.

III. War of The Austrian Succession, 1740–8

The death without male heir of the Austrian ruler Emperor Charles VI in 1740 led to a war begun when Frederick II 'the Great' of Prussia pressed his claim to part of the inheritance. France intervened on behalf of Prussia in 1741 and Britain on behalf of Austria in 1742. In the war France failed to dominate modern Germany and Italy, but conquered Belgium from the Austrians in 1745–7. In Britain, an invasion attempt by the French-backed Bonnie Prince Charlie, Charles Edward Stuart, the son of the Stuart claimant to the British throne, was finally crushed at the battle of Culloden (1746).

IV. The Seven Years' War, 1756–63

This war was an overlap of two conflicts; one between Britain and France (later backed by Spain) and the other between Frederick the Great (r.1740–86) of Prussia and a coalition of Austria, France and Russia. Britain beat its opponents conclusively, while Frederick won a series of victories and successfully checked his enemies. Britain was left in a very powerful situation. As a result, it was able to recover from the loss of what became the United States in the War of American Independence (1775–83) as well as resisting pressure elsewhere from France, Spain and the Dutch.

THE RISE OF PRUSSIA

The rise of Prussia under Frederick II (r.1740–86) owed everything to success in battle. Heir to the brutal Frederick William I, a keen militarist who developed an impressive army, the young Frederick was raised for a military life. Coming to the throne, he rapidly launched the War of the Austrian Succession, successfully invading the Austrian province of Silesia in 1740–1. Frederick's aggressive stance on the battlefield proved decisive, notably against the Austrians at Kolin (1757) and Leuthen (1757) and

The Battle of Quiberon Bay on 20 November 1759 was a crucial naval battle between the British and French navies during the Seven Years' War. The result was the establishment of British naval dominance not just in Europe but around the world.

against the French at Rossbach (1757). In the mid-1740s he developed the 'oblique attack', whereby he concentrated his strength on one side of his attacking line while holding back the other end. This enabled him to deliver a shattering blow and then roll up the opposing line. Prussian domestic policy was focused on preparing for war, but Frederick's system failed against Napoleon Bonaparte in 1806.

GUSTAV III OF SWEDEN

'What is government for?' was a question highlighted by the unpredictable Gustav III (r.1771–92). After the death of Charles XII in conflict in 1718 the monarchy lost power in the Swedish 'Age of Liberty'. In contrast, in 1772 Gustav staged a bloodless coup, aided by widespread dissatisfaction. The powers of the Crown were restored, the Senate was arrested, and the *Riksdag* (Parliament) was reconvened. A new constitution was also approved, with greater powers for the Crown.

One of the most talented of the 'enlightened despots', Gustav's reforms included limited religious toleration, a reduction of the number of capital offences and the reform of the currency. In Rome in 1783, he announced his toleration of Catholics in Sweden. In 1786 he reorganized the Academy of Letters and founded a Swedish Academy devoted to Swedish language and literature, selecting the first members himself and including the leading poets of the period. However, Gustav paid insufficient attention to the need to win élite support and preferred to work with favourites rather than through his council. In co-operation with the non-noble Estates in 1789, he pushed through an Act of Union and Security under which the crown's power to introduce laws was considerably extended. Most public offices were opened to commoners, and peasants' rights to purchase land were extended. In his later years he pursued a bolder foreign policy, leading to war with Russia between 1788 and 1790. On 16 March 1792, an aristocratic conspiracy led to Gustav's assassination.

THE FRENCH REVOLUTION

Rebellions in European states were far from rare in the 16th and 17th centuries, but became so from the 1720s. There had not been a significant rebellion in France since the *Frondes* of the mid-17th century. The French Revolution, which began in 1789, was unusual because it broke out in the centre of government. The initial rebellion became increasingly radical as a result of the failure domestically to secure a settlement and due to the outbreak of war with France's neighbours from 1792.

None of this was inevitable. In the 1770s and 1780s French ministries sought to create a consensus similar to that offered by the British Parliament and to ground French government in institutions that were representative of public opinion, by planning provincial assemblies and then summoning first an Assembly of Notables (1787) and then the Estates General (1789). In 1789, supportive British commentators were enthusiastically discussing the opening stages of what appeared to be a popular and successful revolution that could be compared with the events of 1688 and 1689 in Britain.

Revolutionary France

5 May 1789	*Meeting of the Estates General*
17 June 1789	*Creation of the National Assembly*
14 July 1789	*Storming the Bastille*
26 August 1789	*Declaration of the Rights of Man*
5 October 1789	*Versailles is seized*
1790	*Church property is nationalized*
20–21 June 1791	*Louis XVI flees and is captured at Varennes*
September 1791	*The new constitution is ratified*
April 1792	*War is declared against Austria*
10 August 1792	*Storming of the Royal Palace in Paris*
21 January 1793	*Execution of Louis XVI*
March 1793–July 1794	*The Terror*
7 March 1793	*Vendée Royalist Uprising*
31 May–2 June 1794	*Jacobins depose the Girondins*
27 July 1794	*Coup of 9 Thermidor*
1795	*Creation of the Directory Government*

The Estates General had last met in 1614, and when it convened at Versailles on 5 May 1789, it reflected the distribution of political power in France. There were no peasants or artisans among the representatives of the Third Estate, which effectively comprised bourgeois and middle-class interests. In the spring of 1789 there were hopes of creating a new political understanding, but lacking political skill, Louis XVI proved unwilling to work effectively with those supporting reform. The Estates General became not only a forum for national politics but also a body before which, in comparison with Britain, the government was crippled. The pace of political reform, the urgent desire to create a new constitution, and, crucially, the opposition of powerful domestic elements to the process of reform, and bitter divisions among those who sought change, ensured that it soon became better described as 'revolution'.

The Metric System

In 1790 the French National Assembly adopted a report proposing uniform weights and measures based on an invariable model taken from nature. The idea had been proposed initially in 1673 by Christiaan Huygens, inventor of the pendulum clock, who suggested using the length of a pendulum beating at seconds as the basic unit for a universal measure. In 1790 the French proposed as this unit the length of a pendulum beating at seconds at latitude 45°, midway between the Equator and the Pole. In 1791 the National Assembly adopted as its criterion for the universal measure the metre, or one ten-millionth of the distance from the North Pole to the Equator, as determined from the measurement of an arc of the meridian of Paris between Dunkirk and Barcelona. The standard metre was adopted in 1799 by the International Commission for Weights and Measures in Paris.

Heady oratory, pressure of circumstances, and a growing sense of crisis led the Third Estate on 17 June to declare themselves the National Assembly and to claim a measure of sovereignty as the only elected representatives of the people. Political crisis coincided with a food shortage, and as the price of grain peaked in Paris, the Bastille prison was seized on 14 July in an outburst of popular and violent action. Plans for a royalist counter-revolution were thwarted and the National Assembly abolished all feudal rights and dues and, in the 26 August 'Declaration of the Rights of Man and the Citizen' it claimed that men were free and equal in rights and that the purpose of all political association was to preserve the rights of man. The royal palace of Versailles was stormed on 5 October and Louis XVI taken to Paris.

In 1790 differences over the working of a constitutional monarchy focused on the Church. Church property was nationalized and the Church was turned into a branch of the civil service. The National Assembly imposed an oath on the clergy to support the new order, with dismissal as the penalty for refusal. This divisive step helped undermine support for the revolution in many parts of rural France.

Louis decided to flee abroad and then pursue a negotiated restoration of his authority, but on 21 June 1791 Louis was recognized, stopped at Varennes and returned to Paris. The problem of a monarch out of sympathy with developments in his country led to rising support for republicanism, which increased in April 1792 when war was declared on Austria.

The September Massacres
As well as the storming of the royal palace in Paris, 1792 also saw the massacre of those held in the Parisian prisons, many of them arrested on suspicion of treasonable activities, and rapidly sentenced to death as an aspect of 'people's justice'. Over 200 priests were killed. The massacres helped to unite much European opinion against the revolution. Searching the Classical world for comparisons, the Earl of Dalkeith thought they outstripped 'the massacres of Rome in its most abandoned style'.

To the revolutionaries it appeared crucial to mobilize mass support for a struggle with an insidious but all too apparent enemy: an obvious foreign rival supporting domestic conspiracy and insurrection. These events highlight a singularly modern theme, but one that can also be traced back to antiquity; namely, paranoia driving a rapidly developing language of nationalism, with revolution and radicalization the cause and consequence of this process of struggle.

Creating the concept of a sovereign will of the revolutionary people, to which all opposition was illegitimate, encouraged this fervour. Finally, on 10 August 1792, the radicals took power and the royal palace in Paris was stormed. Louis was seized. The monarchy was suspended by the Legislative Assembly and a National Convention, theoretically elected by universal male suffrage, was established in September. On 21 January 1793, Louis was guillotined.

On 14 July 1789 French rebels stormed the Bastille prison, which held a number of political prisoners. Its fall indicated the beginning of the French Revolution.

As the revolutionary regime struggled with a growing range of foreign foes, it became increasingly radical. The Girondins were replaced in June 1793 by the Jacobins. Using the Revolutionary Tribunal created in March 1793 and the Committee of General Security established in October 1792, and, led by Maximilien Robespierre, they launched a fully-fledged Terror. The regime denounced all obstacles as the work of nefarious 'enemies of the Revolution'. Summary justice led to the death of many royalists as well as those revolutionaries who were seen as insufficiently radical. 'De-Christianization' became a central aspect of state policy.

The Vendée
There was significant opposition to the revolution within France itself. A large-scale royalist rising in the Vendée region of western

France in 1793 was triggered by government attempts to enforce conscription and by the attack on the Church. The rebels called themselves the Royal and Catholic Army. Initial royalist success, which benefited from the advantages of fighting in wooded terrain, led to brutal repression, including widespread atrocities by government forces. This was an aspect of the way in which the Revolution had become a war on the French people.

The Terror inspired fear, but on 27 July 1794 the prospect of fresh purges led to the coup of '9 Thermidor' (named from the month in the revolutionary calendar). Robespierre was overthrown and executed, and a less radical regime took his place. This led in 1795 to the creation of the 'Directory' government. However, the Directory faced considerable international pressure in the War of the Second Coalition, started in 1798.

NAPOLEON

The Corsican general Napoleon Bonaparte, who had made his name with French victories over the Austrians (1795–6) and with the invasion of Egypt (1798), seized power in a coup in November 1799. He became a major war leader, crucially defeating Austria in 1800 (at the Battle of Marengo) and again in 1805 (at the Battles of Ulm and Austerlitz), and also Prussia in 1806 (at the Battle of Jena). His generalship was characterized by an embrace of mobility and by the concentration of force in the attack. Russian forces proved more difficult opponents in 1807 and disastrously so in 1812.

Napoleon became a so-called 'enlightened despot' with singularly few limits. But in his foreign policy he showed a repeated unwillingness to accept compromise, an opportunistic, brutal yet modernizing desire to remould Europe, a cynical exploitation of allies, and a ruthless reliance on the politics of expropriation.

In his attempts to take over Spain in 1808 and invade Russia in 1812, Napoleon failed to understand the situation in either case. The former led

Napoleon Bonaparte seized power in 1799. His reign was marked by unending warfare and rapid expansion, but his decision to advance into Russia led to his defeat.

to an intractable struggle, and the latter to total defeat. In the aftermath of the French army's collapse while retreating from Moscow in 1812, with Prussia and later Austria joining Russia, Napoleon's empire collapsed in defeat in 1813, notably at the Battle of Leipzig. France was invaded in 1814 and with his opponents advancing to Paris and his generals rebellious, Napoleon was forced to abdicate. The Bourbon monarchy was restored in the person of Louis XVIII, the brother of Louis XVI.

In 1814, Napoleon was exiled to the island of Elba off western Italy as part of the Vienna peace settlement, but he escaped in 1815. Evading warships in the western Mediterranean and landing in southern France, he quickly regained control of France, but the European powers were not prepared to accept him back. Napoleon then invaded Belgium, only to be totally defeated by British, Dutch and German (notably Prussian) forces at Waterloo, where the British general, Arthur, Duke of Wellington, proved to be his nemesis. Napoleon surrendered to a British warship, and was then exiled to the distant and British-ruled South Atlantic island of St Helena, where he died in 1821.

THE TREATY OF VIENNA, 1814–15

Napoleon's short-lived return in 1815 interrupted the peace negotiations in Vienna and altered some of their provisions. France was treated more harshly, losing strategic frontier positions and having to pay an indemnity which was enforced by means of an occupation. The successful Allies gained important advantages. Austria was able to dominate Italy, with Lombardy and Venetia under direct rule and Parma and Tuscany under relatives of the Austrian ruler. However, compared to the pre-war situation, Austria had lost Belgium. Prussia gained important parts of western Germany, including Cologne and the Moselle valley, which were designed to act as a barrier to French expansion. Both Austria and Prussia, however, lost gains they had made earlier in the Partitions of Poland (1772–95), with Poland instead coming under Russian rule. Britain made a string of colonial gains around the world, and in European waters it ended up with Malta, Heligoland and the Ionian Islands. Piedmont gained Genoa, while Belgium was ceded to the Dutch ruling House of Orange. Germany remained divided, but among fewer states.

CHANGING GEOPOLITICS

The distinctive feature of the post-medieval European empires was their desire and ability to project their power across the globe: by the late 18th and early 19th centuries Britain was clearly most successful in doing so. This raised an interesting parallel with Russia. In almost every other respect – social, economic, religious, political – the differences between Britain and Russia were vast. However, both powers were, in a way, outside Europe, able to a considerable extent to protect their home base or centres of power from other European states, yet also able to play a major role in European politics. Russian and British geopolitical isolation should not be exaggerated. British governments still had good reason to fear invasion on a number of occasions from 1690 to 1813. Meanwhile, Russia was invaded (by Sweden in 1708–9 and Napoleon in 1812), attacked (such as by Sweden in 1741 and 1788) and threatened (such as by Prussia and Britain in 1791). Nevertheless, their strategic position was different to that of other European states: both had avoided the ravages of the Thirty Years' War, and both were to see off Napoleon and thwart the last attempt before the age of nationalism to re-model the European political space.

CHAPTER 7
INDUSTRIAL EUROPE
1815–1914

The transformation of Europe through industrialization was linked to its dominant imperial and commercial position across the world. Within the continent, the population grew rapidly and more people lived in cities. Politics became more populist as nationalism and representative (male) democracy developed.

THE INDUSTRIAL REVOLUTION

Europe was the centre of industrialization in the late 18th and even more so the 19th centuries, and derived much of the benefit from it. This benefit was uneven, and most concentrated in north-west Europe.

Elsewhere across Europe there was a different story; for example, Portuguese manufacturers were put under pressure from imports from Britain. Yet demand from Europe's growing and more affluent population helped to drive production across the continent. And demand extended as far as more distant regions of Europe such as the Balkans, where it encouraged cotton and tobacco production for markets in the industrial regions.

Coal was the fuel of industrialization, whereas wood required bulk for calorific value and produced poorly controllable heat, making it a poor basis for many industrial processes. In contrast, coal, a readily transportable and controllable fuel with high calorific value, was very useful for manufacturing. Coal could be mined throughout the year, whereas water mills were affected by ice, flooding and summertime falls in water flow. Britain was a key centre of this technological change. By 1750 coal provided 61 per cent of all the energy used in England and produced energy equivalent to that from 4.3 million acres of woodland.

Coal was important to the development of particular industries, especially the iron industry; for example, in South Wales there were 25 furnaces by 1796 and 148 by 1811. Merthyr Tydfil, a Welsh hamlet, became, by 1801, the leading centre of iron production in the world.

Countries and regions that lacked any or much coal, such as Portugal, saw scant industrial growth. A lack of coal also affected the economy in the Netherlands and Scandinavia and was significant in Italy and Spain. In 1880–4 the annual average production in million metric tons of coal and lignite (brown coal) was 159 for Britain and 108 for France, Germany, Belgium and Russia combined. For pig iron (crude iron) the 1880 figure was 7.9 for Britain and 5.4 for the rest of Europe.

Coal fuelled the new technology of railways by powering locomotive steam engines; that is, engines which moved, unlike their stationary 18th-century predecessors. Railways revolutionized transport, but, again, unevenly. Per square mile there were far fewer railways in the Balkans, southern Italy or Spain than in Germany, the Low Countries or Britain.

Similarly, steamships greatly improved sailing times and predictability. The impact of wind and tide diminished, although sailing vessels remained important, not least because they were less expensive to buy and operate. Steamships needed coal and their requirements and capacity led to a focus of trade on a small number of ports with the necessary facilities, such as Liverpool and Bordeaux while smaller ports were marginalized. This process of differentiation was emphasized by the role of steamship–train trans-shipment at particular ports.

NATIONALISM

National consciousness became stronger in the 19th century world and led to nationalism, or the subordination of other values to the idea of a distinct nation occupying a particular area. Stronger states, improved communications, national systems of education, mass literacy, industrialization, urbanization and democratization were each crucial preconditions for nationalism, which was not only an intellectual prospectus, but also a socially comprehensive and insistent mass movement.

There was a symbolic weight to nationalism, as it channelled and fulfilled the ritual aspects of community. Language and literature were presented as resting on a distinct national character, and therefore innate and separate racial characteristics, while on the global scale Europeans were also differentiated from 'others'. Growing belief in concepts such as 'fatherland', 'motherland' and 'homeland' encouraged nationalism.

Nationalism also benefited from the rise of the universal male franchise as it provided a new basis for group dynamics. It legitimized conscription in the military and it intended to blur the old distinction between 'civilian' and 'military'.

1817	Serbia achieves autonomy
1821	Wallachian Uprising
1821–30	Greek War of Independence
1830	Revolutions across Europe
1848	Revolutions across Europe
1848–9	First Italian War of Independence
April–July 1859	Second Italian War of Independence
1860–1	Garibaldi leads the Expedition of the Thousand
1861	Victor Emmanuel II of Piedmont is proclaimed King of Italy as Victor Emmanuel I.
1864	Prussia conquers Schleswig-Holstein from Denmark
1866	Austro-Prussian War
1870	Papal States fall to the new Kingdom of Italy
1870–1	Franco-Prussian War
1871	Kaiser Wilhelm I is crowned as Emperor of Germany
18 March–28 May 1871	The Paris Commune seizes control of the city
1878	Serbia is recognized as an independent state
1912–13	First Balkan War
1913	Albania achieves independence

GREEK INDEPENDENCE AND THE BALKANS

Seriously weakened as a result of defeats by Russia (1806–12 and 1828–9), Turkey was in poor shape to resist growing Balkan demands for independence. Serbia achieved autonomous status in 1817, but in 1821 rebellions in Moldavia and Wallachia (today parts of Romania) failed. However, the rebellion in Greece that also began that year succeeded, largely due to international support, including the Orthodox sympathies of Tsar Alexander I of Russia. The Turks called on Egyptian support, but the Turkish-Egyptian fleet was totally destroyed in 1827 in the Battle of Navarino by an Anglo-French-Russian fleet. This battle helped sway the struggle in Greece, not least because naval support provided opportunities for action against Turkish garrisons.

The Treaty of Adrianople of 1829 ended the Russo-Turkish war and as a result Russia gained control of the mouth of the Danube, Serbian autonomy was achieved, and Russia was allowed to occupy Moldavia and Wallachia until Turkey had paid a large indemnity. In practice, Russian success, which included an advance via Bulgaria as far as Adrianople (Edirne), helped ensure that Greece gained independence in 1830.

This was a far smaller Greece than its modern counterpart. Greece did not gain the Ionian Islands from Britain until 1863 or Thessaly, Crete, and Macedonia, Epirus and the Aegean, all from Turkey, until 1881, 1908, and 1913 respectively. The extensive gains in 1913 were the result of the First Balkan War (1912–13), in which Turkey lost most of its European empire, following on from its extensive losses in 1878. Serbia, Montenegro and Bulgaria also made major gains in that war, while Albania became independent in 1913.

The victors of the first war fell out, leading to the Second Balkan War later in 1913. An isolated Bulgaria was defeated and lost territory to Greece, Romania and Turkey. Anger at its defeat helped explain why Bulgaria joined Germany and Austria in World War I.

THE 1830 REVOLUTIONS

The 1830 revolutions have been overshadowed by those in 1848, but they were significant, not least in creating a new state, Belgium. In 1830 rebellion against control in Italy by Austria and the Papacy failed, as did

The Battle of Navarino of 1827, in which the Turkish fleet was destroyed, was a turning point in the Greek War of Independence.

that in Poland against Russian rule. More serious rebellions occurred in France and Belgium, in each of which the government was overthrown. The failure of the regular troops to thwart the armed rising in Paris in 1830, known as the July Revolution, was in part a matter of the deficiencies of regulars in street fighting. The conservative Charles X of France was unpopular. He was overthrown and replaced by his cousin, Louis Philippe, Duke of Orléans, who ruled what was termed the 'Orléanist' or 'July' monarchy until 1848.

Crisis in one country became an example for others. A rising broke out in Brussels against Dutch rule, and Dutch troops failed to suppress their street-fighting opponents. International intervention eventually forced the Dutch to back down. The resolution of the crisis in 1839 saw Belgium become an independent and neutral state under international guarantee, which was the legal basis for Britain going to war against Germany when it invaded Belgium in 1914.

THE 1848 REVOLUTIONS

In 1848 tensions, including those nationalist in character, within a number of states gave rise to a crisis of governance spreading across much of Europe. From Naples, where revolution broke out in January, the pressure for liberal reform spread in France, Italy, Germany and the Habsburg lands. There were uprisings across Italy, including in Bologna, Florence, Livorno, Messina, Modena, Naples, Rome and Venice.

Nationalist tensions lent particular energy to the rejection of authority in some states, especially Italian hostility to Austrian rule, German opposition to Danish control of Schleswig and Holstein, and Hungarian disquiet about Austrian rule. The Hungarians declared a republic and created a national army. These nationalist tensions ensured that domestic struggles interacted with international divisions.

Some rebellions succeeded alongside others failing. Austria, the multinational empire ruled by the Habsburgs, was the key power in resisting opposition. Nationalism was largely crushed by the Austrians in Italy in 1848, but in Hungary, Russian intervention was important to Austrian success in 1849. In Rome, where Pope Pius IX (r.1846–78) was overthrown and a republic declared in 1849, Austrian, French and Spanish forces restored papal control that year.

In Paris in 1848 the monarchy was overthrown by a popular uprising that led to the foundation of the Second Republic (the first in France had been established in 1792). An uprising by Parisian workers in February forced out King Louis Philippe and the Orléanist monarchy, not least because the elderly king did not want to use regular troops to try to destroy the revolution.

That June, however, when the Parisian workers took to the barricades against the abolition of the national workshops (a form of publicly funded work) they were crushed by the Second Republic's minister of war, General Louis-Eugène Cavaignac. There was a clear geographical and social edge to the struggle, with Cavaignac using peasant regular troops and national guardsmen to fight his way through the city's barricades against the insurgents' 'Army of Despair'.

The beneficiary of the crushing of radicalism was Napoleon's nephew, Louis Napoleon, who was elected President of the Second Republic that December. He consolidated his position with a coup in December 1851 and became Emperor Napoleon III (r.1852–70).

ITALIAN AND GERMAN UNIFICATION

Nationalism led to state formation, in particular transforming Italy (1860–1) and Germany (1866) into political units. In each case the defeat of Austria, a multi-national empire ruled by the Habsburg dynasty, was a key element. Italy was organized around the kingdom of Piedmont and Germany around that of Prussia, but both claimed their role in terms of new nation states.

Prussia won a series of sweeping victories over Denmark (1864), Austria (1866) and France (1870–1). In addition, the defeat of Austria, notably at Sadowa/Königgrätz, was matched by that over Austria's German allies, including Hanover, Hesse-Cassel and Saxony, which meant that Prussia came to dominate Germany. The two-power system in Germany, with Austria being the senior, disappeared. Rather than seeking *revanche* (revenge) in Germany, Austria increasingly pursued a Balkan destiny, which made it possible to negotiate an alliance with Germany. France suffered because the pool of recruits for the German army became greater with Prussia's annexations.

In 1870 the poorly-led French were heavily defeated by the Prussians in the first month of the war, but the war continued. Emperor Napoleon III of France surrendered at Sedan, only to be replaced by the Third Republic and a Government of National Defence. The Germans then besieged Paris and shelled it into surrender. France surrendered in 1871, with Prussia annexing most of Alsace and much of Lorraine, a key industrial zone. Victory enabled Prussia to transform her hegemony within Germany into a German empire ruled from Berlin.

Nationalism led also to agitation for independence against imperial rule, especially in Poland and Finland against Russia, in Ireland against Britain, and in the Balkans against Turkey. Indeed, the development of democratic ideals both helped nationalism and opposed imperial states.

The Paris Commune, 1871

The violent seizure of control of Paris in March by mostly working-class radicals led to a full-scale assault by the army of the new republican government. The Commune's decrees ranged from the separation of church and state to the abolition of night work in bakeries. After extensive street fighting, in which about 10,000 Parisians were killed, the Commune was suppressed in May. About the same number who had been captured were promptly shot.

In southern Italy after unification with the north, strong resistance remained in Naples and Sicily to the new Italian regime, which was regarded as alien. Opposition was so pronounced that, in 1866, when 18 year olds were conscripted to fight Austria, those from disaffected Naples and Sicily were excepted. In 1860 an army under Victor Emmanuel II of Piedmont combined with a volunteer force under Giuseppe Garibaldi, a much-travelled revolutionary, to overthrow the Neapolitan Bourbons. Garibaldi and 1,000 red-shirted volunteers sailed from Genoa to Marsala to help a revolt in Sicily against the Bourbons. After defeating a Neapolitan force at Calatafimi, Garibaldi captured Palermo following three days of street fighting. He defeated the remaining Neapolitan forces

The Prussian king, Wilhelm I, was crowned German Emperor in the Palace of Versailles at the conclusion of the Franco-Prussian war, in a humiliating experience for France.

on Sicily at Milazzo and, having crossed the Straits of Messina, marched north to defeat the Neapolitans at the Volturno and to capture Naples. Meanwhile, Victor Emmanuel II had marched south from Bologna, winning battles at Castelfidardo and Macerone against the small papal army and the Neapolitans respectively. Garibaldi handed his conquests to Victor Emmanuel, enabling the latter to become the figurehead of the new kingdom of Italy.

In Spain support for the Carlists, conservatives who resisted the government in Madrid, drew on local loyalties, especially in Navarre and upland Catalonia. In the Balkans, and more generally, much activity still focused on subsistence or was only for the local economy. This was true of agriculture and industry, and greatly affected the collective psychology of the population.

The Fall of Rome
The ending of the old order was clearly demonstrated in 1870, when the Papal States of central Italy were successfully invaded by the

new Italian army. This signalled a major collapse in the power of traditional Catholicism. Although the Church retained the support of much of its flock, its institutions were considerably weaker and the fabric of Counter-Reformation Catholicism had been destroyed. This was a long process, in which the policies of secular nationalist governments in the second half of the 19th century was only the final stage. Earlier there had been inroads, first at the hands of Enlightenment governments and then as a result of the policies of the French revolutionaries and their clients.

RUSSIA UNDER THE TSARS

Russia changed rapidly in the century before the revolutions in 1917. The 19th century saw large-scale industrialization, agricultural development, urbanization and the end of serfdom by Alexander II in 1861, the last affecting over 23 million people. There was a radical opposition, which led to the assassination of Alexander II in 1881. However, that opposition was a marginal force. Indeed, there was no large-scale rebellion, unlike in the two proceeding centuries. There was a process of change despite the conservatism of Alexander III (r.1881–94) and Nicholas II (r.1894–1917), but not at the pace seen in Germany.

Culturally, there was a strong division between westernizers and slavophiles, one that involved the past as well as present (and the future). Peter the Great was hero to the former and villain to the latter, his reputation a way to advance the debate over Russia's identity and culture.

Russification was actively pursued in the empire. Large (Russian) Orthodox cathedrals were built in Helsinki and Tallinn. The cathedral in Tallinn, built on a prominent site between 1894 and 1900, was a clear display of cultural power. The cathedral was dedicated to Prince Alexander Nevsky, who had defeated Swedish and German (Teutonic Knights) forces in 1240 and 1242 respectively, and who had been canonized by the Orthodox Church in 1547.

THE CRIMEAN WAR, 1854–6

International power politics played the key role in causing this war, for nationalism was not the only source of conflict. Russian expansion at the expense of the Turks, notably via a major naval victory off Sinope in 1853, offended France and aroused British concerns about a threat to the overland route to India. Napoleon III, Emperor of France, saw this as a way to strengthen his domestic position. He had only recently replaced the Second Republic.

The wide-ranging war came to focus on Sevastopol, Russia's naval base in Crimea, which was a threat to the Turks in the Black Sea. Technology, in the shape of steamships, telegraphs and new rifles, played a role in the fighting. All sides found their armies inadequate, which helped to drive reform. The Russians' failure punctured the impression of their proficiency, which had prevailed since the failure of Napoleon I's invasion in 1812.

IMPERIALISM AND THE SCRAMBLE FOR AFRICA

Imperialism drew on a range of interacting factors. Crucially, the seizure of territory by expanding empires became normative and, as victory and conquest became easier, expansionism and a sense of superiority toward non-Europeans were encouraged. In addition, economic opportunities appeared more tempting in an expanding and yet also increasingly integrated world economy, one fired by a quest for raw materials and markets.

Imperialist activities were designed in part to pre-empt rival powers and, as a result, European power politics was contested around the world. For example, Britain moved into Sudan in part to stop French expansion from the *sahel* belt into the valley of the Upper Nile, while Portuguese, British and German expansion in southern Africa entailed trying to thwart similar attempts by the other powers. Russia and Britain competed in Afghanistan and Iran, and Britain and France in South-East Asia.

THE ECONOMY OF THE LATE 19TH CENTURY

New products, such as cars, pharmaceuticals and telephones, provided opportunities and posed problems of adaptability. Many of these consumer products required new investment, which was readily available, and were more dependent on skill and technology than some of the older 'metal bashing' industries that had been crucial to the first Industrial Revolution. The balance of industrial power altered with the rise of Germany, which by 1914 had forged ahead of Britain in iron and steel production, and was also particularly successful in chemicals, electrical engineering and optical goods. By then, however, America's output was equivalent to that of the whole of Europe, which was thus falling behind in terms of its (admittedly large) relative share of the world economy.

Agricultural production within Europe was affected by trans-oceanic production, notably of grain in North America, beef in Argentina, mutton and wool in Australia, and lamb in New Zealand. This was assisted by steamships which brought capacity and speed, and by rail systems overseas. These imports greatly hit Western European production, and led to a focus there on goods that were not imported long-range, such as milk and vegetables.

For industry, the ratio of value to bulk encouraged trade, both long- and short-range. Links within and between the economies of the individual countries grew. Developments in one country tended to be shared, which was particularly true of the recession of 1873–96, which succeeded the earlier period of general growth.

CHANGING SOCIETIES

Across Europe, hierarchical societies and their values coexisted with rapid social change. These brought social dislocation, instability and anxiety, expressed in part by hostility to immigrants. Deference and traditional social patterns ebbed. Privilege coexisted with meritocratic notions. Greatly expanded institutions that, within limits, reflected such notions – the civil service, the professions, the universities, and the armed forces – played a role in the creation of a new social and cultural establishment different from the traditional aristocracy; although least so with armies. At the same time, working-class political consciousness and activism developed markedly and was characterized by a sense of international solidarity. In cities, public education and, later, low-rent housing programmes were designed to cope with the disruption of urbanization and social change.

TECHNOLOGY

Technology had become a freed genie in the 19th century, and the cumulative character of change was more apparent. Railway and telegraphy were succeeded by the motor car and telephone, electricity and the wireless. Innovations such as powered, manned flight, were preceded by attempts to achieve these innovations. The growth of the genre of 'scientific romance', as in the work of Jules Verne and H.G. Wells, for example, testified to the seemingly inexorable advance of human potential through technology and its impact on the collective imagination.

The 19th-century fascination with the machine remained strong and influenced both popular and high culture, including the new form of the cinema. The *Manifesto* issued by Emilio Filippo Marinetti in 1909 and the *Manifesto of Futurist Painters* that followed in 1910 launched the artistic movement Futurism as a creed of science expressed in part through glorification of the machine. *391*, the magazine of the avant-garde Dada artistic movement, launched in Barcelona by Francis Picabia in 1917, presented images of machines as symbols of life.

CHAPTER 8
EUROPE AT WAR
1914–45

Europe was the epicentre of the two world wars. Vast numbers of soldiers died, as did millions of civilians, particularly in World War II. New political systems, such as fascism and communism, took hold, while society and culture changed dramatically.

THE ROAD TO WAR

There was nothing inevitable about the route to war in 1914. Bellicosity and armaments had not led to war in recent years, even during the crises related to the Austrian annexation of Bosnia in 1908 and the Balkan Wars of 1912–13. However, in 1914 the alliance systems in place in Europe ceased to act as a deterrent to action. Instead, these alliances transmitted anxiety about shifts in international geopolitics and national politics. This was particularly true of Austro-Hungarian concern about the position in the Balkans. The assassination there, in Sarajevo, Bosnia, of the Archduke Franz Ferdinand, heir to Emperor Franz Josef, provoked the determination to punish Serbia in a misplaced attempt to produce stability in the multi-ethnic empire. This brought in Germany on Austria's side, and Russia on Serbia's.

As alliances moved toward war, the Franco-Russian alliance led Germany to attack apparently more vulnerable France in order to weaken Russia and, in doing so, German forces advanced through neutral Belgium, which brought its guarantor Britain into the war. Far from 'sleepwalking' into a major conflict, all the powers understood that this would be a serious and costly struggle. However, none appreciated how major or how long.

WORLD WAR I

The terrible casualties of the conflict, about 9.45 million deaths, including about 2 million in Germany, 1.8 million in Russia, and 1.4 million in France, have contributed to a later perception that its heavy costs made it pointless. In fact, although at great cost, the aggressor powers were finally defeated and in a shorter period than many major wars before it.

Much of the subsequent fighting took place on the Western Front in France and Belgium, but the war also encompassed extensive fighting in Eastern Europe, the Balkans, north-eastern Italy, the Middle East and Germany's overseas colonies. The German-led alliance proved successful in Eastern Europe and the Balkans, overrunning Serbia in 1915 and most of Romania in 1916. Russia was brought low in 1917 by a revolution that owed much to strains caused by a war in which Germany was repeatedly successful. The following spring, Russia's new Communist rulers negotiated peace on German terms. However, on the Western Front, German offensives in 1914, 1916 and 1918 failed to bring success.

 Allied soldiers advance during the Battle of Passchendaele with air support.

The Face of War, 1915

'I lit a cigarette and tried to pretend I wasn't frightened to death. And just then a man ran by with his arm nearly off. I was so afraid he would bleed to death that I lost my fear for a minute or two and followed him, stood in the trench and dressed him. Lewis my corporal was cowering down by my side in a small scoop. I wouldn't let him come out, as I told him one of us was enough at a time, when suddenly a shell exploded on him and blew him to pieces, knocked me over and broke the leg of a stretcher bearer who was two yards further off than I was. I don't know why I wasn't killed. My nerve went and I would have bolted only I heard the poor beggar hit in the leg calling for me so I groped my way to him and dressed him. I have never been so shaken... literally sick from shock, then... broke down.'

– Captain Hugh Orr-Ewing, Medical Officer, writing to his fiancée from the Battle of Loos.

The length of the war arose partly from the time taken to develop tactics able to restore mobility to the Western Front and partly from the time necessary to ensure the provision of sufficient munitions. The balance of resources was also important; the Germans ran out of reserves of troops in 1918, in part due to their heavy losses during the Spring Offensive of that year, and in part because they did not move sufficient troops back from the Eastern Front after the Communists, having taken over in Russia, ended their war on German terms in the Treaty of Brest-Litovsk.

Two Battles of World War I

Verdun, 1916
Seeking to break French will, the Germans attacked at Verdun. They planned to advance rapidly on a front of their choice to capture

territory, which the French would then suffer heavy losses trying to retake. Verdun, a fortress in the Meuse Valley in north-eastern France, had great symbolic significance for the French, and they took heavy casualties without their willpower breaking. The offensive both cost the Germans heavily and served no strategic purpose. In campaigning that lasted from February to December 1916, the French lost 378,000 men and the Germans 336,000.

The Somme, 1916
Aiming to take pressure off the French at Verdun, a British-dominated offensive on the Somme was launched on 1 July, but proved disastrous as machine gun fire, from defences that had not been suppressed by artillery fire, was responsible for about 21,000 British deaths alone. Further attacks did not break through, and in the end, by late November, the offensive had cost about 420,000 British and 200,000 French casualties. At the same time the Germans lost possibly half a million men, as Allied attacking techniques improved.

In contrast, the Allies had a fresh source of troops as a result of American entry into the war in 1917. They played an important role in 1918. They would have done even more so had the war continued into 1919. American aid was also crucial to the British and French war economies.

Moreover, in late 1918, when strongly attacked on the Western Front, the Germans failed to display the resolve and persistence offered earlier, and at very heavy cost, by the French and British. In part this was because of the strains in the German alliance system and on the home front. The key element, however, was the defeat of the German army on its main battlefront, a defeat different from, but equivalent to, that of the *Wehrmacht* by the Soviet army in 1944. The British focused on improving artillery firepower and accuracy, so as to dominate the three-dimensional battlefield and apply firepower more effectively than in earlier attacks.

Improved artillery–infantry co-ordination was also significant. Defeated and retreating, the Germans asked for and received an armistice in November 1918.

THE PEACE OF VERSAILLES

In the peace treaty signed at Versailles (1919) following World War I, Germany lost territory to France, Poland, Belgium and (neutral) Denmark, while its overseas colonies were all handed over. The Hohenzollern dynasty had already fallen with defeat in 1918 and Germany then became a republic. Reparations (compensation for wartime damage) were decreed on the pattern of the reparations the Germans enforced on France in 1871. The peace terms were designed to prevent Germany from launching new wars, and thus to provide collective security for Europe. Under the supervision of the Inter-Allied Military Control Commission, the size and equipment of the German military were seriously restricted. Germany also had to accept an occupied zone along the French and Belgian frontiers and a demilitarized zone beyond, the net effect of which was to end the possibility that the River Rhine could provide a strategic defensive frontier for Germany.

Germany was stigmatized by a war guilt clause and by the insistence that German officers be tried for war crimes, especially the treatment of Belgian civilians in 1914 and the consequences of indiscriminate submarine warfare. The Allies had wanted war criminals extradited for trial before an international tribunal but in 1920 agreed, instead, to the German request that the trials be held before the Supreme Court in Leipzig. Only 17 of the Allies' list of 853 alleged war criminals were tried.

The peace terms were fair, given the role of German aggression in helping start the war, but were to be misleadingly treated as an outrage by critics. In practice the terms were far less onerous than those that followed World War II, terms generally regarded as successful in maintaining peace. In 1919 the victors adapted to practicalities as well as to ideological concerns; Germany had not been overrun by the Allies while, as a result of her earlier defeat of Russia, she was still in occupation of large territories in Eastern Europe when the war ended. In 1918–19 the victorious powers were determined to try to prevent the spread of Communist revolution from Russia to Germany. Talk in France of a Rhineland separated from Germany led nowhere.

The Habsburgs also lost their imperial throne. Austria and Hungary became small states, while Italy gained some territory, Romania gained Transylvania, Czechoslovakia became independent, and Serbia expanded to become Yugoslavia. Newly-independent Poland gained territory from Russia, Germany and Austria. Bulgaria lost some territory to Greece and Romania. Turkey had to accept occupation of much of the country, but in 1922–3 was able to bring that to an end in a successful nationalist struggle of independence that involved a heavy defeat for Greece.

WOMEN AND THE VOTE

Successive extensions of the right to vote in the 19th century were initially restricted to men. Modern standards of equality were a long way off, even in countries that considered themselves progressive. The notion of 'separate spheres' was well-established, and women's special role was generally defined as that of home and family.

This situation was under challenge by the early 1910s, notably from suffragettes in Britain. However, their success was limited. Instead, the world wars had a major impact by leading to more women entering the labour force, altering social assumptions and practices, and in encouraging the expansion of the right to vote. Social mores were affected by a wartime decline of deference and also by the rapidly shifting role of women in the militarized wartime societies. With men called to fight, the economic sphere extended for women, and notably in industry, especially so for Britain. In addition, large numbers of women and children replaced rural male workers. Furthermore, many women accompanied the military as nurses. Whereas only 72 army sisters had been employed in British military hospitals in 1898, a total of 32,000 women served as military nurses in 1914–18. Air attack put women into the front-line of casualties. At a far larger scale, many were left as widows by war, including 600,000 in France during World War I.

Britain gave women the vote in 1918 (and on an equal basis in 1928), although France did not follow suit until 1945. However, the election of women to national assemblies, and their appointment to senior government positions, was uncommon before the second half of the century. Margaret Thatcher became Britain's first female prime minister in 1979 and Angela Merkel became German chancellor in 2005. Italy is yet to have a female prime minister, or France to have a female president, although the runner-up in 2017 was a woman, Marine Le Pen.

THE RUSSIAN REVOLUTION

Russia had already experienced a revolution against the background of military defeat by Japan in 1905, but that was on a small scale and readily suppressed. In contrast, the strain on Russian society was far greater in World War I. The organizational weakness of the Russian state was especially clear in transport and food allocation, and the resulting pressures were concentrated in the cities, where demand for food was greatest.

Food shortages became more serious in the context of a rising public paranoia that drew on a lack of national unity and on related political and social tensions, with 'speculators' supposedly holding the populace in thrall while 'Germans,' including the Tsarina, betrayed them. In practice, the 'betrayal' linked to the Germans was that obtained by their skilful use of subversion, notably arranging the transportation of the Bolshevik (Communist) leader, Vladimir Ilyich Lenin, to Russia in April 1917. Alongside popular discontent there was significant discontent among the élite, focused not only on Nicholas II but also on Tsarism.

A popular demonstration in St Petersburg against the price of bread on 8 March 1917 focused tension, but the police failed to control it and the government turned to the army. Disaffected, the troops on 12 March refused to fire on the crowds and, instead, went on strike. The following day, the troops and the factories elected representatives for a 'soviet' or council. In the face of mounting chaos some politicians and generals thought it necessary to act, and did so by determining to get rid of Nicholas II. He abdicated on 15 March, bringing the Romanov dynasty and monarchy to an end, and the *Duma* (Parliament) established a provisional government. This event is usually known as the February Revolution, as in the Old Style Julian calendar, the revolution lasted from 23 February to 3 March.

This unleashed political debate but did not solve the problems of a state that could not wage war effectively, nor of a society under tremendous pressure. The war, moreover, went on, although without success. Indeed, the eventual fall of the new government in November 1917 owed much to its failure to win success on the battlefield; or, alternatively, to pull out of the war altogether.

The Bolshevik influence in the St Petersburg Soviet increased and on 7 November a coup led to the overthrow of the government, with little resistance. The government was unable to rely on the military because the willingness to fight on against the Germans compromised military co-operation. At first there was a Bolshevik-dominated coalition government, but the Bolsheviks rapidly seized complete control of the government. In the spring of 1918 the Bolsheviks launched a drive for power leading to a civil war that lasted until 1921.

 Vladimir Ilyich Lenin addresses the crowd in Red Square during the October Revolution of 1917. Lenin was the leading figure in the Bolshevik movement.

The forces opposed to the Bolsheviks in the civil war included not only Whites (Conservatives) and, at times, Greens (peasant armies), as well as rival forces on the left, but also those of non-Russian peoples who had separatist agendas of their own; for example, Ukrainians and Finns. In addition, there were foreign forces opposed to the new regime, including from Britain, France, Greece and Romania. In combination this was a formidable array, but it was divided. In addition the White forces fought badly and proved unable to win and sustain peasant backing. The Bolsheviks also benefited from having controlled Moscow and St Petersburg and from fighting on interior lines. They ruthlessly mobilized resources and used violent terror to suppress opposition.

World Revolution?
In the situation of great flux that followed World War I, major efforts were made to spread the Communist revolution. Institutionally, this belief was expressed in the Comintern, or Communist International, created in 1919. A series of Communist parties was founded. In March 1919 a Communist-led government under Béla Kun won power in Hungary and proclaimed it a Soviet republic. However, the Romanians, with Czech support and French backing allied to Romanian conservatives, overthrew the revolution that summer. Communism was also checked elsewhere in Europe in 1919, notably in Germany. The Communists were not to gain control of an independent state until 1940, when Soviet forces occupied the Baltic Republics: Estonia, Latvia and Lithuania. The democratic appeal of Communism was very limited, as the Communist leadership appreciated.

The Bolsheviks succeeded in defeating their opponents and in regaining control of Ukraine and the Caucasus, but failed with Finland, Estonia, Latvia, Lithuania and Poland, each of which became independent. Tsar Nicholas II and his family were murdered by the Communists in 1918.

From the outset, the Communists believed in a utopian ideology, extreme and organized violence, atheism, and the rejection of preceding Russian history. During the civil war and the 1920s, the Orthodox Church was crushed, with the slaughter of tens of thousands of priests and monks, and the desecration and destruction of churches, monasteries and the tombs of saints. As a consequence, the real and spiritual landscapes of Russia and the psychological life of the people were transformed.

STALIN

Lenin died in 1924, to be replaced by Josef Stalin. A paranoid figure who was happy to embark on mass murder, Stalin pushed through his vision of modernization. State control was used to direct industrialization and to impose collectivization (state control) on agriculture. The Orthodox Church was further devastated, while Muslim courts and schools were suppressed. The government controlled information, so that the people lived in the shadow of propaganda as well as terror. There was a major expansion of the industrial sector and of electricity generation, but at a heavy cost in terms of living standards.

During the 1931–3 Soviet famine, about three to five million people died in Ukraine, as well as two million in northern Kazakhstan and southern Russia. Soviet policies towards the Ukraine famine, which was, to a degree, a result of deliberate acts, led to claims of genocide, both from within Ukraine and elsewhere; claims that were frequently expressed once Ukraine became independent in 1991. The Soviet census of 1937, the first for 11 years, was suppressed and the officials involved were executed, probably because it revealed losses through famine earlier in the decade, which according to the government had not occurred.

Stalin's perceptions of inevitable, imminent war generated his policies of breakneck modernization. Frustrated by the persistent gap between intention and implementation, the regime in the 1930s adopted more radical and totalitarian impulses and initiatives. These led, in the purges that began in 1937, to the slaughter of much of the military and economic leadership. Stalin's rival, Leon Trotsky, who was exiled in 1929 and murdered at Stalin's behest in 1940, referred to the dictator as leading to 'a river of blood'.

Stalin brooked no dissent as he sought to modernize the Soviet state. The results were always harsh and often disastrous.

INTERWAR EUROPE

Recovery after World War I and the post-war disorder underwrote a European system in the 1920s that was generally peaceful and, with many governments, democratic. The Communist challenge was contained, although the rise of right-wing authoritarianism was seen in Italy, Portugal and Spain. Far from the post-war peace settlement sowing the seeds of a new war, as frequently claimed, the international system it established actually worked better in the 1920s (at least from the perspective of western interests) than was generally appreciated in the 1930s. There was domestic instability, as there was prior to 1914, but also less international tension than then.

The peace settlement was also followed by a series of international accords designed to prevent conflict, notably the Locarno Agreement of 1925, which provided for a mutual security guarantee of Western Europe and, earlier than many could have expected in 1918, re-assimilated Germany into the international system. In the 1920s there was a strong interest among the European powers in a viable and consensual international order.

To argue that Versailles led to the rise of Hitler is therefore inappropriate. Hitler rejected Versailles and the international system it sought to create, but the responsible *realpolitik* of the 1920s, which entailed compromise and benefited from the idealistic currents of that decade's international relations, focused on another German, one far more prominent in the period, Gustav Stresemann, the Foreign Minister from 1923 to 1929. Without the failure, protectionism, misery and extremism produced by the Depression from the 1930s, the 1920s order would likely have continued.

THE GREAT DEPRESSION

The financial crisis that began with the Wall Street Crash of 1929 was followed by a major slowdown of the world economy. Governments increasingly thought and planned in national, rather than international, economic terms. This led to a measure of corporatism, as governments sought to direct both labour and capital, and this was conducive to a closer integration of economies and national policies. In contrast, globalism was negatively affected by the political and ideological potency of nationalist economic views, and by the resulting protectionism. It became more difficult to export or to obtain capital and technology from abroad.

Europe was hard hit. Unemployment grew greatly, as did under-employment. By 1934 about 10.7 per cent of the Italian male workforce was unemployed. In addition, thanks to fewer opportunities elsewhere emigration became more difficult. The Depression hit confidence in democratic systems and encouraged a turn to totalitarianism. By 1938 the sole democracy in Eastern Europe was Czechoslovakia.

THE RISE OF FASCISM

Dissatisfaction with the post-World War I peace terms was accompanied in Italy by severe economic problems, including rising unemployment. The major political parties could not co-operate, and a 'Red Scare' caused by concern about Communism was exploited by Benito Mussolini, who founded Fascist squads to fight it. Fascism showed a violent anti-leftism and a willingness to ally with the élites. It also drew on hostility to liberalism among intellectuals and others who disliked the masses and parliamentary democracy. The different tendencies of Fascism left it unstable and disorganized, reliant on rhetoric to try to provide cohesion. Mussolini himself saw rhetoric as an aspect of the emotion and enthusiasm that was necessary to lead the masses, not least radical nationalism. Lacking popularity and even apparently purpose, the government succumbed to Mussolini's seizure of power in 1922, dubbed the 'March on Rome': in fact Mussolini, like many other Fascists, went by train.

The Rise of Extremism

1922	*Mussolini seizes power in the March on Rome*
1923	*Hitler leads the unsuccessful Munich Putsch*
1928	*Mussolini abolishes elections*
1929–39	*The Great Depression*
1933	*Hitler becomes Chancellor of Germany*
1936–9	*Spanish Civil War*
1936	*Hitler remilitarizes the Rhineland*
March 1938	*Anschluss between Austria and Germany*
October 1938	*Sudetenland is assigned to Germany*
March 1939	*Germany invades Czechoslovakia*
September 1939	*Germany declares war on Poland, beginning World War II*

Once in power, Mussolini took control of much of the state, and in 1928 he abolished elections. Opposition was suppressed by intimidation, imprisonment and violence. Propaganda was used to help disseminate a grandiose image of great achievement. There was a commitment to force, notably in the conquest of Ethiopia in 1935–6, and no sense of limits nor of the economic weakness of Italy.

The Spanish Civil War

The right-wing Nationalist victory in a bitter civil war in 1936–9 was the consequence of a right-wing military uprising against the Republican government. This did not succeed as well as originally planned, and instead led to a struggle in which the Republicans continued to hold much of the country until their rapid collapse in early 1939. Both sides drew on international support, notably Germany and Italy for the Nationalists and the Soviet Union for the Republicans. The civil war saw the terror bombing of cities, notably of Guernica by German aircraft. The victorious Nationalist leader Francisco Franco, a general, then became dictator. Opposition was ruthlessly suppressed.

HITLER

The post-war crisis in Germany was overcome in 1919 and a democracy established in the form of the Weimar Republic. This lasted until 1933 and provided both economic recovery and a measure of political stabilization. The extremes were contained, as when Adolf Hitler and his far-right group the Nazis tried and failed to stage a coup in Munich in 1923. Weimar was subsequently regarded as a failure, but it was a successful liberal society in the difficult circumstances of post-war defeat.

Weimar, however, broke down in the aftermath of the Great Depression. The Nazis did well in elections and also benefited from the divisions between the other politicians. Hitler was able to become Chancellor in January 1933 and rapidly introduced a Nazi monopoly of power. Rather than responding to the fiscal strains of 1934 by restraining rearmament, Hitler pressed ahead. The Four-Year Plan, initiated in 1936, was designed to ensure self-sufficiency and readiness to go to war in four years. That year he also unilaterally remilitarized the Rhineland, in defiance of the Versailles peace settlement. Britain and France did not respond.

Hitler pressed on in March 1938 to occupy Austria, uniting it with Germany in the *Anschluss* (union). This was a fundamental redrawing of

the map of Europe. He moved on to demand from Czechoslovakia that it hand over those areas with a majority of Germans, the Sudetenland. Under the threat of war, the Czechs, abandoned by Britain and France in the Munich agreement with Germany and Italy, gave in.

On 15 March 1939, Hitler occupied most of Czechoslovakia, breaking the agreement he had made in Munich. In response, on 31 March Britain and France guaranteed Poland and Romania against German attack. This, however, was undercut by the Molotov-Ribbentrop Pact between Germany and the Soviet Union of 23 August, a non-aggression agreement between both states that greatly expanded German opportunities. When Germany invaded Poland on 1 September 1939, Britain and France followed by declaring war on 3 September.

WORLD WAR II

The rapid German success in Poland in 1939 was followed, far more surprisingly to contemporaries, in the spring of 1940 by the German conquest of Denmark, Norway, Luxembourg, the Netherlands, Belgium and France. All bar France were neutral, and aggression was the German motivation, although strategic advantage was also gained by these conquests. For example, Norway provided bases for use in naval conflict with Britain.

British forces were pressed into desperate retreats from Norway and France in 1940 and Britain itself was subject to air attack and to the threat of invasion. This also marked the end of limited war because the new British government under Winston Churchill was not interested in a compromise peace dictated by a victorious Germany, which was, indeed, on offer. This decision meant that the conflict would continue until the actions of these other powers played a decisive role.

The Neutrals

In both world wars there were many neutral powers, although not all were able to sustain their neutrality in the face of attacks or pressure from the combatants. Spain, Sweden and Switzerland were neutrals in both world wars. In World War I, so also were Denmark, the Netherlands and Norway, but all three fell victim to unprovoked German attack in 1940. Now independent of Britain, Ireland was neutral in World War II. The neutrals also suffered from the disruption of war, as well as more direct damage such as the sinking of ships by submarines as the combatants sought to enforce blockades.

German success owed much to taking the initiative and to the mobility of airborne and tank forces. However, it was made possible by serious flaws in the strategy of opponents and by the co-operation of the Soviet Union. By allying with Hitler, Stalin proved more than willing to subordinate the cause of international Communism to that of state-expansion in concert with Germany. Both Hitler and Stalin rejected liberal capitalism as a domestic agenda for liberty and freedom and as an international agenda focused on opposition to dictatorial expansionism. A total of 1.17 million Poles were deported to *gulags*, or Soviet labour camps, and many others were slaughtered.

 A German soldier armed with a machine gun waits in Norway during Operation Weserübung, the invasion of Denmark and Norway in 1940.

For Hitler, however, war with the west was only a stage to his determination also to destroy Communism. On 22 June 1941 he launched Operation Barbarossa, the invasion of the Soviet Union. This was initially successful, and the Soviets suffered heavy losses of territory and manpower in late 1941. However, the deficiencies already seen with German operations were to be compounded by the vastness of the territory that had to be conquered, as well as by the availability of massive Soviet reserves. Lulled by over-confidence in the value of a swift offensive, by their quick success over France in 1940, and by their tactical and operational skills and ability, the Germans had not planned or prepared adequately for the conflict. By embracing their harsh racial beliefs the Germans both underestimated the Soviets and brutalized them.

A German Europe

The Nazi leadership planned a 'New Order', with an enlarged Germany including not only Austria and much of Czechoslovakia but also territorial gains from Yugoslavia, Poland, France, Belgium and Luxembourg. This would be central to a new European system of subject territories under German administration (such as Norway), territories under German occupation (such as Serbia), and territories under allies, and with the Germans at the top of a racial hierarchy. Thus, Ukraine was to be devoted to SS estates supported by subjugated peasants. The economy of Europe, both conquered and allied, was to be made subservient to German interests. The rest of Europe was to provide Germany with forced labour, raw materials and food, and to receive German industrial products on German terms. New transport links were to be constructed.

German forces were stopped in December 1941 short of their targets of Moscow and St Petersburg, then attacked again in 1942 from 28 June only to suffer again from an ill-conceived and poorly-executed plan.

Defeated at Stalingrad in a Soviet counter-offensive in the winter of 1942–3, the Germans failed again when they attacked at Kursk in July 1943.

This failure resulted in a crisis in confidence within Germany, one to which the overthrow of Hitler's ally Mussolini and the heavy British bombing of Hamburg contributed greatly. In turn, Hitler manipulated a toxic cocktail of fanaticism and terror in order to keep the Germans in the war. Resistance in Germany was limited. The most serious instance was the July Bomb Plot of 1944, but this conspiracy of army officers failed to kill Hitler and was rapidly suppressed.

In 1944 Germany faced all-round assaults. The Soviets drove the Germans back in Eastern Europe and the Balkans, Anglo-American forces landed in France, notably in Normandy on D-Day on 6 June, and reconquered both it and Belgium, and the Germans were battered by unprecedented Anglo-American air attacks. These air attacks greatly weakened the German war economy and hit morale.

In 1945 German defeat was total. Soviet forces advanced into Germany from the east and Anglo-American forces from the west. Hitler committed suicide as the Soviets fought their way into Berlin, and Germany surrendered unconditionally.

THE SLAUGHTER

The attack on civilians was most brutally seen with the German genocidal mass murder of about six million European Jews in the Holocaust, a product of Hitler's racial paranoia and hysteria. Anti-Semitism led some (but not all) of Germany's allies to co-operate fully with this mass murder, especially Romania, but the key role was that of Germans (which at this point included Austrians). There was no secret in Germany about the war on Jews. Much of the killing was at or near where Jews lived, notably in Eastern Europe, but there was also the movement of Jews to concentration camps, where they were mistreated and worked to death, and to extermination camps, where they were killed at once, notably by means of poison gas. At the most deadly camp, Auschwitz II, about 1.5 million Jews were slaughtered. At other camps, such as Treblinka and Sobibor, hundreds of thousands were killed.

Wannsee

Senior Nazi administrators and SS leaders meeting at a suburban villa at Wannsee on the outskirts of Berlin on 20 January 1942 helped co-ordinate the organization of what was intended as a 'Final Solution.' At this 'conference' they resolved that all European Jews, including those not hitherto under German control, were to be deported to death camps and slaughtered. The SS took a central role.

Particular effort was designed to ensure that there was no Jewish future and therefore no children. Nearly 1.5 million Jews under 14 were killed in the Holocaust. So also with pregnant women.

The German slaughter of other civilians was also heavy; for example, 120,000 Poles were killed in Warsaw in 1944, in large part in suppressing the Warsaw Rising and in the related slaughter of civilians. The killing of civilians by all powers, through bombing and other military acts, did not compare in intention or action with German mass murder, but, nevertheless, it was devastating.

THE HOME FRONT

As with World War I, World War II led to a large-scale mobilization of national resources, a massive extension of the powers of government, and an attempt to regiment and direct society. At the same time, for all combatant nations there were major concerns about morale and resilience, which encouraged attempts to gather intelligence, as well as to ensure that the 'home front' was kept supplied with food and opinion. Propaganda played a key role, not only with news but also with the arts, including film and music. In the Soviet Union, history was searched for suitable instances of exemplary nationalism. The large numbers of men who fought ensured that Britain and the Soviet Union relied heavily on women workers. Germany, however, preferred to rely on the slave labour of those it had conquered.

For occupied countries the war was bleaker, as resistance was treated harshly. Thus, in France, where German occupation from 1940 was initially largely peaceful, the situation became more violent from 1941. Across Europe, resistance was easiest in mountain and forest terrain.

Resistance to German occupation was an important diversion of German resources and inflicted damage on German communications. German methods proved self-defeating. Both its ruthless approach and the lack of adequate resources for security made it difficult to conduct an effective occupation policy.

CHAPTER 9
POST-WAR EUROPE

1945 to the present

The threat of a nuclear conflict combined with a realignment of international politics, ideological division and the fear of repeating the events of the first half of the century led to a tense atmosphere during this period. Europe changed greatly as population growth, technological development, urbanization and a range of new cultural mores and environmental concerns made the continent a very different place.

CHANGING EUROPE: THE NEW SETTLEMENT

The peace settlement saw major territorial, demographic and political changes. The first two have substantially lasted to the present. With its forces in Berlin, Vienna, Budapest and Prague, the Soviet Union was a major winner. It retained all of the gains it had obtained in 1939–40 (from Poland, Romania and Finland, as well as the Baltic Republics in their entirety). The Soviet Union also added part of Czechoslovakia that had been annexed by Hungary in 1939, as well as the northern part of the German province of East Prussia.

The (southern) remainder of East Prussia went to Poland, which also gained extensive German territories on its western frontier, namely Silesia and Eastern Pomerania. However, Poland lost more extensive territories (about 48 per cent of pre-war Poland) on its eastern frontier to the Soviet Union. This outcome reversed the Polish gains of 1920–1 and was rejected by the exiled Polish government. Today, as a result of the disintegration of the Soviet Union in 1991, these territories are parts of Belarus, Ukraine and Lithuania. Poland, in the meantime, had moved westwards as a country.

Territories and cities were renamed accordingly. The German city of Breslau, where a long resistance to attacking Soviet forces had been mounted in 1945, became the Polish city of Wroclaw. Königsberg, the capital of East Prussia, became Kaliningrad, honouring a Soviet politician. Other names that entered the dustbin of history included Silesia, Pomerania and Stettin.

There was also a large-scale movement of people. In 1945–6 nine million Germans fled or were driven west from the territories acquired by the Soviet Union, but, even more, from pre-1939 Czechoslovakia, Poland and other countries. Poles were moved out of the territories gained by the Soviet Union in western Ukraine and were resettled in lands cleared of Germans. This was 'ethnic cleansing' in operation. Violence was involved, but not genocide. There was a determination to avoid the post-World War I situation of sizeable ethnic minorities within the new nation states.

THE BEGINNING OF THE COLD WAR

Josef Stalin's anti-western paranoia had remained strong even when he was allied with Britain and the United States, and the end of World War II was followed by a resumption of pre-war rivalry. The Soviet determination to dominate Eastern Europe was a key cause of tension. The focus of later confrontation between Soviet-led and American-led forces was Europe. Indeed, many of the arms, both nuclear and non-nuclear, were deployed in Europe and/or focused on targets there.

Concerned about Soviet expansion, America proved far more engaged with Europe than had been the case after World War I. Large-scale financial assistance, known as Marshall Aid, was generously given in order to assist economic regeneration. In addition, in 1949, with the creation of the North Atlantic Treaty Organization (NATO), the USA (and Canada) committed themselves to the security of Western Europe. The new alliance included much of Western Europe, including former neutrals – notably the Netherlands, Denmark and Norway.

The Cold War

1944–9	*Greek Civil War*
1947	*Marshall Plan proposed*

24 June 1948– 12 May 1949	*Berlin Blockade*
28 June 1948	*Josip Tito is expelled from the Cominform*
4 April 1949	*Creation of NATO*
5 March 1953	*Death of Stalin*
14 May 1955	*Establishment of the Warsaw Pact*
23 October– 10 November 1956	*Hungarian Revolution*
4 June– 9 November 1961	*Berlin Crisis*
15 October 1964	*Nikita Khrushchev is replaced by Leonid Brezhnev as ruler of USSR*
5 January– 21 August 1968	*Prague Spring*
12 August 1970	*West Germany and the USSR sign the Treaty of Moscow*
July–August 1975	*Helsinki Accords*
1980–1	*Solidarity movement in Poland*
June 1987	*Mikhail Gorbachev announces the policies of glasnost and perestroika*
9 November 1989	*Fall of the Berlin Wall*
16–27 December 1989	*Nicolae Ceauçescu is deposed in the Romanian Revolution*
23 August 1990	*German Reunification Treaty*
26 December 1991	*Dissolution of the Soviet Union*

American forces were deployed accordingly, including aircraft in Britain, Italy and Spain, troops in West Germany, and warships in Britain and Italy. In 1947 America replaced Britain in supporting the royalist government in Greece against the Soviet-backed Communist insurgency. American aid helped the royalists succeed in 1949, a process encouraged by division in the Communist camp when Yugoslavia, under Josip Tito, broke away from Soviet Union control. Spain under the Franco dictatorship was not part of NATO, but America's concern to anchor Spain in its alliance system led to an agreement under which the Americans deployed aircraft from Spanish bases. Indeed, a new geopolitics led to new American base requirements, including in Iceland and Greenland. From 1952 Greece and Turkey were members of NATO, despite the British preference for a NATO focus on Western Europe and the North Atlantic.

In opposition to NATO the Soviet Union dominated Eastern Europe, where, in 1955, it established the Warsaw Pact. This included Poland, Czechoslovakia, Hungary, Romania, Bulgaria and, from 1956, East Germany. Individual states, whichever bloc they were in, were given a role by the rivalry, rather than having important issues of their own, including specific geographical and political concerns and characters.

The Fate of Germany

Germany's defeat in World War II led to its destruction as a political structure. Unlike after World War I, it was divided between a Soviet zone of occupation, which became the German Democratic Republic (or East Germany, a Communist dictatorship) and American, British and French zones, which became the Federal Republic of Germany (or West Germany, a democracy). Two very different states were founded in parallel, which lasted until unification in 1990. One laid claim to being anti-Fascist, anti-imperialist and Communist, while the other was democratic, market economy-based, and western.

Stalin's assertiveness and determination to control lead to defeat for his plans in Yugoslavia in 1948 and in Berlin in 1949. In 1948, as a result of Stalin's quest for ideological conformity and for control over policy, the governing Yugoslav Communist Party under Josip Tito, its wartime leader, was accused of abandoning Communist principles and of failing to follow Moscow's lead on foreign policy. Tito's removal was called for and the Soviets organized an economic blockade of Yugoslavia, began a propaganda offensive, and started small-scale armed attacks.

The Berlin Airlift

Isolated within the Soviet occupation zone, Berlin was itself divided between the four powers that had occupation zones in Germany. This situation appeared to challenge the Soviet position. In the Berlin Crisis, the Soviets blockaded West Berlin (the American, British and French zones) from June 1948 to May 1949. This was met by an impressive and successful Anglo-American airlift of 1.5 million tons of supplies. The crisis appeared to bring war near, but it led to the stationing in Britain of American bombers. The threat of the use of the atom bomb helped bring a solution to the crisis, and the Soviets dropped their attempt to take over the city.

 An American plane brings supplies to Berlin in 1948 as civilians watch.

The offensive failed, however, in large part because the wartime Communist movement in Yugoslavia had been less dependent on the Soviet Union than those elsewhere in Eastern Europe (with the exception of Albania). Moreover, Yugoslavia had no common border with the Soviet Union. First Secretary of the Yugoslav Communist Party from 1937, Tito was also Prime Minister and President of post-war Yugoslavia until his death in 1980.

The turn against Tito helped poison the political atmosphere in the Soviet bloc as a whole. From 1949 there were show trials across the bloc of those deemed Titoists and accused of nationalist deviationism. They joined the list already occupied by Trotskyites.

The murderous pursuit of alleged internal dissidents weakened the Communist movement and lessened popular support for it. The crisis and the subsequent show trials showed that the Communist bloc was not going to be able to act as a united bloc in a comparable way to that of the less ideologically coherent West, because the emphasis on uniformity turned difference into disobedience or dissent.

THE END OF EMPIRE

From the end of World War II the Western European colonial powers rapidly abandoned their colonies. They were affected by independence movements in these colonial territories, but also by a new lack of commitment to empire that in part arose from the exhaustion produced by the recent world war. In the late 1940s Britain abandoned what became India, Pakistan, Sri Lanka, Myanmar and Israel, the Dutch left Indonesia and the French left Syria and Lebanon. Although the French left Cambodia, Laos and Vietnam in 1954, the period 1950–6 saw the retention of most colonies, although in 1957–64 Britain and France abandoned the overwhelming majority, and Belgium left Congo. Later, in 1975 and 1976, there was a fresh wave of decolonization, notably in Africa, following the overthrow of right-wing regimes in Portugal and Spain, for example of Angola and Mozambique. The Cold War played a role in the decolonization struggle. This reflected the Soviet attempt to leap beyond the existing system of Western 'containment.'

THE LONG BOOM

The period from 1945 to the oil price spike linked to the Yom Kippur War in 1973 was one of rapid economic development that was subsequently called the 'Long Boom'. By the 20th century there was a more integrated system not only spanning the world but also affecting societies far more intensively than before. Free trade and readily available investment, in a new economic order established by the Americans led to a major increase in productivity and growth. The application of new technology in manufacturing and agriculture led to important productivity gains. Mechanization, such as the use of tractors, resulted in the movement of workers from the land, especially in France and Germany. In manufacturing, the employment of mass production in new purpose-built factories permitted a more effective introduction of new technology and organizational methods. Britain, France and Italy developed mixed economies with much state planning and nationalization alongside the continuance of the private sector. Protectionist and corporatist Spain and Portugal saw only modest economic growth.

West Germany grew faster. This owed much to the economic liberalization pushed by Ludwig Erhard, Federal Chancellor from 1963 to 1966 (and earlier an influential economics minister) and other leaders. Influenced by liberal-minded economists, the West German government adopted pro-competition policies and fostered currency stability. The West German economic and financial system contrasted with the nationalizations and state control seen in France and Britain, and especially with the total state control in Communist East Germany, where growth rates and living standards were far worse than in West Germany. West Germany also benefited from the skill of its engineering industry, as well as from harmonious labour relations.

RESISTANCE TO THE SOVIET UNION

The cruel, inefficient and dictatorial nature of the Soviet bloc led to popular uprisings despite the extent to which Communist control rested on a police state and massive surveillance. The most important uprisings in the 1950s and 1960s occurred in Hungary in 1956 and Czechoslovakia in 1968. Each was suppressed by Soviet military action, in part because the Soviets believed that any attempt to reform Communism would unravel the entire bloc. In each case the Soviets were backed by other Communist-bloc countries. As an example of the use of divisive paranoia for political ends, some Warsaw Pact troops were told that they were being deployed into Czechoslovakia in order to stop a NATO invasion. In fact, a key element of each crisis was a lack of Western intervention. This helped contain what might otherwise have become a more serious east-west crisis. The same was the case in Poland in 1981, when the suppression of the popular reforming Solidarity movement by the Polish army did not lead to a wider response. However, these steps greatly helped to discredit Communism for at least that generation.

THE KHRUSHCHEV YEARS

Nikita Khrushchev, the First Secretary of the Communist Party from 1953 to 1964, won the power struggle that followed the death of Stalin in 1953, and he led the Soviet Union from 1955. Keen to encourage labour morale to secure popular support, Khrushchev sought to focus economic growth on living conditions to a degree not seen under Stalin. Socialist consumerism was on offer. Moreover, in 1956 Stalin was denounced for brutality and for allowing a personality cult to develop around him. This was followed by Khrushchev overthrowing his rivals in the Party in 1957. He was removed from power by the Central Committee in 1964 on the grounds that he had risked war over Berlin (1961) and Cuba (1962), but also because of his failure to secure an increase in grain production.

THE BERLIN CRISIS, 1961

The building of the Berlin Wall in early August 1961 provided an apt symbol of the lack of freedom to which Communist government gave rise. The open border between East and West Berlin had offered an easy means for fleeing from East Germany, and by building the wall the Communists abandoned any suggestion that their system was more popular. Their division of the city was initially with barbed wire, but later with a concrete wall supported by frontier troops trained to shoot would-be escapees, and ready to do so. This division was a breach of the agreements between the citizens of Berlin to move freely through the whole city.

In response the crisis escalated at the international level and there was a stand-off in Germany between American and Soviet tanks in October. The end result was a Berlin Wall that left the divided city as a powerful testimony to hostility. The wall was also a declaration that East Berlin was in the Soviet zone and that German reunification was highly unlikely to occur. The Berlin Wall became a powerful and repeated subject and motif in fiction and film.

THE CZECH CRISIS, 1968

Economic failure in Czechoslovakia contributed to a call for political reform and in 1968 the Stalinist leader Antonín Novotný was replaced by Alexander Dubček, who called for 'Socialism with a human face' and a 'new start to Socialism'. To the concern of the Soviet Union and other Communist states, this 'new start' involved a dilution of Communist control; indeed, the 'Prague Spring' saw both an abolition of censorship

 American and Soviet tanks face off at Checkpoint Charlie on 29 October 1961 in the Berlin Crisis.

and increased freedom of speech. The Soviets were also concerned by a failure to consult Moscow and by the impact of developments on nearby parts of the Soviet Union.

The Czech reformers insisted that, unlike Hungary in 1956, Czechoslovakia would remain loyal to the Warsaw Pact and that the 'leading' role of the Communist party would be retained. However, doubts led to an invasion in August 1968 by Soviet, Polish, Hungarian, Bulgarian and East German forces. The suppression of the Czech reform movement was followed by the reimposition of a police state.

RADICALISM AND '68

Student protest proved a key element in a major upsurge in radical action in 1968, with the students moving to the left. To some commentators there were echoes of the Year of Revolutions in 1848.

More generally, the '68 movements touched all Western European

 Soviet soldiers attempt to make their way past the crowd of protesters in Prague during the crisis of 1968.

191

countries in many ways, and had, as their basic cause, anti-authoritarianism, specifically the clash between young people, with new purchasing power and expectations, and gerontocratic power structures, including the family, school, business (presented as capitalism) and government (seen as the authorities). There was also an echo of these movements in Eastern Europe, although liberalism in Czechoslovakia, in the shape of reform Communism, was crushed in 1968 by Soviet military intervention.

The radicals in Western Europe failed to appreciate that in criticizing and seeking to demolish established systems and institutions, such as the nuclear family, there was frequently nothing much to take their place. More positively there was an extension of democracy as more power was given to young people and women. Indeed, 'women's liberation' was a key theme of the period.

The short-term political repercussions of 1968 were limited, which encouraged some to resort to more radical ideas, and even terrorist movements in Italy and West Germany. The institutional expression of the demands for change had proved weak and far from durable. Demonstrations were no way to challenge the police when the latter enjoyed the acceptance, if not backing, of much of society. Moreover, radicalism in the military was limited, unlike in Russia in 1917 or Portugal in 1974. Partly as a result, Portugal, where the right-wing dictatorship in power from 1926 was overthrown in the 'Carnation Revolution' by radicals in the army in 1974, was to witness more radical change than France, Italy or West Germany in or after 1968. Politically, the 1960s ended with conservative governments still in power in France, Italy and West Germany, and gaining power in Britain in 1970.

The Paris Riots, May 1968

In May 1968, student occupations and demonstrations in Paris led to a brutal response by the riot police that escalated into a crisis, including general strikes across France. Assured of military support if necessary, Charles de Gaulle, however, regained the initiative, encouraged by popular support and by the divisions among his

> *opponents. President Emmanuel Macron found it difficult to retain control in 2018 in the face of violent demonstrations in Paris.*

OSTPOLITIK

Willy Brandt, the Social Democratic Party leader, became West German Chancellor in 1969 and promoted a new approach of *Ostpolitik*. Under earlier Christian Democrat-dominated governments, there had been a refusal to consider *détente* with the east until the division of Germany and frontier disputes with Poland had been addressed, but this policy had failed to deliver results. Brandt hoped that an improved relationship would bring stability and enable West Germany to take a more central role in Europe. *Ostpolitik* also reflected a degree of assertion based on impressive West German economic growth, and was a product of the search for a political alternative to the arms race. In 1970 West Germany signed treaties with the Soviet Union and Poland, in effect recognizing the existing borders. A treaty with East Germany in 1972 meant recognition of the latter as an independent state. Although tension in Europe was reduced, *Ostpolitik* also stabilized the Communist regimes without bringing much liberalization.

THE HELSINKI ACCORDS, 1975

Ostpolitik helped prepare the way for the Helsinki Accords of 1 August 1975, a European-wide process of stabilization that included the USA and Canada as a counterweight to the Soviet Union. The preparatory talks began in November 1972 and the final summit was on 30 July 1975. The Helsinki Accords accepted existing borders and non-intervention in the internal affairs of other states. Although there were remarks about human rights and fundamental liberties, the Soviet Union, like other Communist regimes, was adept in preaching rights while practising autocracy. However, the combination of stabilization, rights, and a European common space did provide a window of opportunity for dissidents in Eastern Europe. In both east and west, *détente* in part reflected a decline in the power and authority of the former and of deference in the latter.

Solidarity

Poland in the early 1980s proved a lightning rod for the unpopularity of Communist rule, with the added ingredients of traditional hostility to Russia and a strong national Christian commitment. Large-scale strikes in 1980 were precipitated by an increase in the price of meat, but the establishment of an unofficial trade union, Solidarność (Solidarity), challenged the authority of the government and were of concern to other Communist regimes. The Soviet defence minister supported intervention, but his colleagues were reluctant to do so, while the Soviet Union was warned not to act by US President Ronald Reagan. Instead, the Polish army imposed control under martial law in 1981. Solidarity's leaders, as well as thousands of others, were detained without trial, and many were killed.

FRANCO'S SPAIN AND ITS FALL

General Francisco Franco's authoritarian right-wing regime lasted in Spain from his victory in the civil war of 1936–9 until his death in 1976. This was a socially conservative dictatorship. It also changed, in line with more general developments in Europe. For example, in the 1960s there was an embrace of capitalism not seen earlier and a degree of liberalization. This situation looked toward the dismantling of the dictatorship that followed Franco's peaceful death and the rapid introduction of democracy. A reactionary coup in 1981 rapidly fizzled out but indicated the role of chance in political events; as did the instability in Portugal in 1974–5 that followed the overthrow of the authoritarian right-wing regime in 1974.

STAGNATING SOVIET LEADERSHIP

The sluggish and complacent Leonid Brezhnev (ruled 1964–82), who replaced Nikita Khrushchev as the Soviet Union's Communist Party leader, failed to see the need for change, neglected warnings of problems and proved particularly negligent in economic management. The regime was increasingly characterized by incompetence, corruption and sloth.

The failure to match Western European improvements in living standards and the sham character of Communist progress contributed to the widespread apathy, cynicism and disillusionment among the population. The inherent weaknesses of the Communist system, and notably its economics, were increasingly brought to fruition.

Even so, the strength of the dictatorship helped keep it in power, based on a process of surveillance and coercion that was linked to a fatalist sense among the public that there was no alternative to Communist rule.

Brezhnev was succeeded by the 68-year-old Yuri Andropov, the head of the KGB. He understood the need for improvement but had no idea of how to ensure it, except by pressing for better social and work discipline. This did not work and, in any case, he was increasingly ill. When he died in February 1984, Andropov was replaced by Konstantin Chernenko, another old and ill figure who died on 10 March 1985. Chernenko lacked even Andropov's intellect. This appointment contributed to an acute sense of policy deadlock.

The Soviet dream had failed. The combination of economic difficulties, political sluggishness, and a much better-educated Soviet citizenry indicated that the country in 1985 was very different to what had been called for during the 1917 Revolution.

THE FALL OF SOVIET COMMUNISM

Mikhail Gorbachev, who became Soviet leader on 11 March 1985, brought a new generation to power and sought to create 'Socialism [Communism] with a human face'. However, attempts to introduce market responsiveness to a planned economy, in yet another stage of encouraging Communist consumerism and thus winning popular support, proved impossible. Economic reform, in particular *perestroika* (restructuring), which involved the loosening of much of the command economy, led unexpectedly to economic problems, including inflation, shortages, a breakdown in economic integration, and demands for political change.

Supporting *glasnost* (openness) in government and society, Gorbachev was confident that the Soviet Union and the Communist Party would not only be able to survive the challenges of change, but would be mutually strengthened by them. He was to be proved totally wrong.

Gorbachev made it clear that no military support would be provided to the Eastern European Communist governments. This helped lead to their collapse in 1989, and to multi-party politics and free elections. The collapse of Communist control in East Germany proved dramatic, but was matched elsewhere. There was no significant resistance to the changes other than in Romania, where it was overcome. In 1990 East Germany was reunited with West Germany.

Romania in 1989

The Romanian dictator Nicolae Ceauşescu sought to use force to suppress anti-Communist demonstrations, both in Timişoara, where tanks were sent in, and in the capital, Bucharest. There, on 21 December a popular demonstration in the face of an address by Ceauşescu was attacked by the Securitate, *the secret police, and over 1,000 people were killed. The following day, renewed demonstrations led Ceauşescu to flee. The army eventually acted in support of the demonstrators, providing enough force to overawe the Securitate and to overthrow the regime. Ceauşescu was detained, tried and shot by the army.*

The process spread to the Soviet Union, which was dissolved in 1991, as the former republics within the federation, such as Ukraine, gained independence. In some of the non-Russian republics, nationalism had long provided a popular and inclusive language and form of dissent. From mid-1988, the growing weakness of the Soviet state, and the division and confusion of the government's response to nationalism, was accentuated by the strength of nationalist sentiment, especially in the Baltic republics, the Caucasus republics and western Ukraine. This sentiment had been manifested from the mid-1980s in increased opposition to Communist rule.

When the republics declared their independence, Gorbachev supported the attempt to maintain the authority of the Soviet Union by sending troops into them in January 1991. This led to clashes in Riga and Vilnius, but did not intimidate the nationalists. Nationalism culminated when Boris Yeltsin, the head of the Russian Federal Socialist Republic, launched a Russian nationalist movement against the remaining structures of the Soviet Union.

The Fall of the Berlin Wall

The Berlin Wall was opened on 9 November 1989 and this was seen as a symbol of a new age. The fall of the wall, which was soon demolished, became a totemic act, like that of the Bastille in Paris at the outset of the French Revolution in 1789. Large numbers of East Berliners poured over the border and the pressure for reform in East Germany was increasingly supplemented by demands for German unity.

Responding to these events, there was an attempted coup in Moscow by hard-line Communists on 19 August 1991 seeking to stop the process; however, in the face of popular demonstrations they were unable to prevail. Hardline Communists were marginalized and the republics opted for independence. In December 1991 most joined the Commonwealth of Independent States. The Soviet Union ceased to exist. From the 2000s Russia, under an authoritarian Vladimir Putin, sought to claw back its loss of power, intervening militarily in Georgia in 2008 and in Ukraine repeatedly from 2014.

YUGOSLAVIA IN THE 1990s

Yugoslavia, another Communist federal state, was affected in the 1980s by many of the same problems as the Soviet Union, including economic stagnation, nationalist feeling and uneasiness about the position of the prime power, in this case Serbia instead of Russia. In 1990 free elections in Croatia and Slovenia helped to strengthen their opposition to Serb assertiveness, and in 1991 they declared independence. The resulting conflict between Serbs and Croats spilled over into Bosnia, a part of Yugoslavia that was ethnically mixed, with large Croat, Serb and Muslim populations. Each of the communities formed an army. The conflict was brutal, involving the deliberate targeting of civilians.

Western intervention to end the conflict was initially undermined by a combination of American reluctance to act, not least from the military leadership, and European weakness, both military and political. The latter included marked disunity over the desirability of action.

Nevertheless, settlements were eventually imposed in Bosnia in 1995 and in Kosovo in 1999, at the expense of the expansionism and ethnic aggression of a Serbian regime that unsuccessfully looked for Russian sponsorship. The crises showed the strength of ethnic tension in the Balkans and led to a new language of conflict focused on 'ethnic cleansing'.

The tensions within European culture, notably the fault-lines of ethnic and religious animosities, were readily apparent. This was a lesson most Europeans did not wish to learn, but one that remains relevant. It has been rewritten by the consequences of large-scale immigration from outside Europe.

RELIGION

Christianity did not collapse in Western Europe. It declined, but there were still many committed believers. However, for both most believers and for the less or non-religious, faith became less important. Permissive 'social legislation' flew in the face of Church teachings and left the churches confused and apparently lacking in 'relevance'. There were political battles over divorce, contraception, homosexuality and abortion, as the influence of the Catholic Church was contested. It lost, not least due to referenda in favour of change, as with the strongly-contested legalization of abortion in Portugal (2007) and Ireland (2018).

Responding to social and intellectual currents, the Catholic Church showed a willingness to follow new paths, such as a modernized liturgy, in 1962 when Pope John XXIII (r.1958–63) summoned the Second Vatican Council.

However, the Church's hold over many of its communicants was lessened by widespread hostility towards the ban on artificial methods of contraception in the 1968 encyclical (papal letter) *Humanae Vitae*. Markedly conservative tendencies were also seen with the first two non-Italian popes in modern times, the Polish John Paul II (r.1978–2005) and his German successor, Benedict XVI (r.2005–13). His Argentinian successor, Pope Francis (2013–), is the first pope from outside Europe since the 8th century Syrian Gregory III.

Conservative influences were challenged by liberal theologians, most prominently Hans Küng, a Swiss Catholic priest, professor of theology at Tübingen University and adviser to the Second Vatican Council. He became a leader of liberal Catholicism, accusing John Paul II of turning the Church against the Second Vatican Council and toward extreme conservative doctrines.

In Eastern Europe and Russia, atheism was the official position of the communist regime, but many continued to cling to Christianity. For countries trying to respond to Soviet hegemony, such as Poland and Lithuania, Christianity provided a powerful sense of identity and spiritual meaning. After the fall of the Soviet Union in 1991, Russian Orthodoxy revived rapidly as a public force. Vladimir Putin found it politically expedient to woo the Church in the 2000s and 2010s. In Yugoslavia, religion combined with (and helped to define) ethnicity to cause a bloody and protracted series of conflicts. Catholic Croats, Orthodox Serbs, and Muslim Bosnians and Kosovars, proved the major protagonists.

Spiritualism enjoyed a marked revival, and from the 1960s both 'new age' religions and Buddhism appealed to many in Western Europe. They proved better able than the churches to capture the enthusiasm of many who wished to believe, in a material world where faith had become just another commodity. Traditional non-Christian faiths, including Islam, Judaism and Hinduism, had only a limited appeal to Christians. Instead, these faiths essentially catered there for immigrant groups and their descendants.

THE CHANGING ENVIRONMENT

Changes to animal habitat due to human action over the last century, and particularly as a result of economic growth, was greater than that over any century in the previous two millennia. The century witnessed an accelerating race between humans and other animals for profit from what humans saw as their habitat, but which was also, of course, that of animals.

The idea of the world as a terrain to shape, and a commodity to be used, was challenged from the 1950s by the proposition that it was a biosphere, operating in an organic fashion and using natural feedback mechanisms to sustain life. The globe was now increasingly presented as an environmental system affected by human activities, such as atmospheric pollution, which affected the feedback mechanisms. The working of this system was increasingly clarified by the spread of environmental concern and knowledge. Thus, it became possible to track and dramatize the movement of airborne or waterborne pollutants.

Population growth, economic development and greater affluence all put pressure on the environment. The assault from pollution was varied. Carbon dioxide emissions rose from burning forests or fossil fuels, 'acid rain' damaged woodland and hit rivers and lakes. Lead emissions from traffic seriously affected air quality. The consumer society produced greater and greater quantities of rubbish, much of it non-biodegradable and some of it toxic. Environmental damage as a consequence of accidents was important. Moreover, noise and light pollution became more serious and widespread. Plastic waste in the seas (for example, plastic under which fruit and vegetables were increasingly grown in Spain dumped in the Mediterranean) entered the human food chain via algae and fish.

Anxiety about environmental pressures led to demands for sustainable development. This proved a nebulous concept, difficult to define and enforce, and one that was contested by local communities anxious for jobs, companies keen to maximize revenues, and governments focused on development. Nevertheless, 'Green' activism and then political movements became more significant from the 1960s, across Europe. Green politicians benefited in particular from proportional representation systems, as in Germany, but even entered Parliament in Britain. Far from being a fad, 'Greenery' became more prominent, not least as concern about global warming increased and also, in the 2010s, with greater sensitivity to the impact of plastic, notably in the oceans.

CULTURE

Encouraged by the role of American films and television programmes, and of American-derived products in consumer society, notably cars, the mystique of America as a land of wealth and excitement grew greatly in the 1950s, especially in Western Europe, much of which, notably West Germany, was reshaped in response to American influences and consumerism. From the 1960s youth culture came to the fore. This brought self-styled personal liberation, a situation that has continued to the present.

The contraceptive pill influenced social practices and, to an extent, norms, especially for women. Sex was separated from procreation and then from marriage. Demands for the recognition of an independent sexuality focused on heterosexual activity with an assertion of women's rights to enjoy sex, to have it before marriage without incurring criticism, and to control contraception and thus their own fertility. This offered many women greater control over their life, although the situation was less benign for many women. Abortion became another stage in the struggle for control while lesbianism was affirmed as an option.

Feminism became culturally and politically significant anew in the 1960s, although the feminists of that era tended to underplay earlier efforts. In practice, feminism had many different strands and some clashed with others. Social changes combined with a self-conscious women's movement to produce, at least for some women, a gender resolution. The number of married women entering the job market escalated, and more women returned to work after having children. In part, feminism related to the subsequent tension over the rights and remuneration of these women: trade unions and management had very much rewarded male skills. The legal position of women also improved, while equal rights were enshrined in institutional practices.

For some, female self-consciousness developed in a more political direction. This, however, did not match the experience of all women. Indeed, there were significant class tensions, with working class women often feeling neglected in the 'consciousness raising' approach.

Images of masculinity were also in flux. The decline of manual work, and the growing prominence of women workers, both contributed to a sense of change; indeed, in some contexts, it imperilled masculinity. Traditions of respect bound up in the fact of work and the hierarchies of employment were challenged. So also with the decline of patriarchal patterns of control. These were overthrown in the case of wives, daughters and sons, but also abandoned by many fathers.

Different attitudes to homosexuality were separate, but part of the equation of social change. The gay rights movement presented homosexuality, which had hitherto been treated in many countries as a crime, as normal and deserving equal treatment with heterosexuality. This led to legal and social changes and to high profile statements, such as when Bertrand Delanoe, a self-proclaimed homosexual, was elected Mayor of Paris in 2001.

EUROPE IN THE NEW MILLENNIUM

The early 2000s began in a benign atmosphere, with the end of the Kosovo crisis in 1999 suggesting that post-Cold War instability had been successfully overcome. This optimism was seen with the successful adoption of the Euro as a common currency by many European Union member countries.

The situation became far less benign as a consequence of the financial crisis that began in 2008. This put pressure on the economies of European countries and notably on those that had a high national debt, particularly Greece, Portugal and Italy. The Euro lessened the ability of countries to manage their own finances. Germany benefited greatly from the open markets of the EU, but this was far less the case for many other countries, notably in Mediterranean Europe.

Politically the crisis encouraged the European Commission and France to press forward the cause of further EU federalism. However, this course was also widely opposed, contributing greatly to a sense of political volatility. Tension was readily apparent between nation-states on the one hand and the combination of supranational bodies, notably the EU, and sub-state regions on the other. The latter were particularly favoured by peoples whose nation-states were recent and weak, for example Belgium and Italy, as opposed to Britain, Denmark and Scotland.

It is possible to exaggerate the effectiveness of the nation-state. There is a kind of circularity: the nation-state represents national interest effectively because its very existence *defines* those interests. What is less clear is that the interests thus defined and pursued by the nation-state are the primary interests of the people of that state.

At the same time, the nation-state continued to play a role, whether inside, separate, or outside the European project, as represented by the EU. At the same time, the nation-states faced problems, as could be seen in 2019 with the Treaty of Aachen signed by France and Germany in order to provide shared defence, foreign and economic policies. In practice, this treaty, which very much expanded on the 1963 treaty between the two states, was a response to a drift of politics moving against the wishes of their leaders, President Macron and Chancellor Merkel.

Aachen is heavy in symbolism because of its role as Charlemagne's capital. Its choice was emblematic of the 'deep history' offered as populism and nationalism were debated, defined and redefined. Populism and nationalism were certainly of increasing influence across Europe in the late 2010s and neither focused support on the EU.

CHAPTER 10
THE FUTURE OF EUROPE

A number of issues face Europe in the years to come, including falling population growth, rising immigration, and questions over the direction of the EU. At the same time, long-lasting tensions over the boundaries of Europe are likely to continue, and the countries of the region must decide how they will interact with the outside world, all as climate change provides new and pressing challenges.

DEMOGRAPHICS

The future of Europe and that of the current Europeans may not be the same but they are certainly linked. Much of the continent today is affected by zero population growth. A fall in the number of children per family has been countered to a degree by longer life expectancy, but this fall has affected many communities. It is a product of a range of social changes including a marked rise of the female workforce, as well as by assumptions about desirable family size.

The impact of traditional religious norms has fallen in both Catholic and Protestant Europe. Contraception has become normal, and abortion and homosexuality legalized. These, and other, social and cultural changes have cut down the size of families, while more young people are not marrying or are postponing having children. As a result, the demographic pattern in Europe looks very different to other parts of the world. Italy, Spain and Portugal, all Catholic countries, have particularly low population growth. Without immigration, the population of much of Europe would be static, if not falling; and from the 1990s the percentage of the world's population living in Europe fell dramatically. There was also a rise in the elderly dependency ratio, one that put pressure on the rest of society.

IMMIGRATION

The demographic situation makes immigration a more visible and apparent issue, particularly in the context of a rapid and unprecedented rise of the world's population in recent decades. This rise is set to continue from about 7.4 billion today to maybe 10.75 billion by the end of the century. That rise will be most rapid in Africa, where it is due to reach 3 billion. Africa is only separated by the Mediterranean, which is easy to cross. Indeed, immigration from Libya to Italy became a major issue in the politics of the latter in the mid-2010s.

The consequences of large-scale population growth elsewhere are likely to include immigration into Europe at an unprecedented rate. In part, that has already occurred, altering the demographic, ethnic and religious structures and patterns of societies across Europe and notably so in southern Europe.

Rates of migration rose in the 20th and 21st centuries in response to pull and push factors. The pull factors came in the forms of economic opportunity, news of this opportunity and improved transport routes; the push factors from armed conflict, political, ethnic or religious persecution, poverty often linked to population growth, and natural disasters, such as droughts and floods.

Patterns of migration were varied and complex. Most was not into Europe but within it and, indeed, within countries, in particular from countryside to city, and to areas of greater opportunity, for example from former heavy industrial areas in north-eastern to southern France, such as the Toulouse area, and from northern England to the south.

Changes in agriculture, from mechanization and international competition, also proved significant. Thus, in Italy, there was large-scale migration from Sicily and the south to northern industrial cities such as Milan and Turin. In Portugal, the small peasant plots in the north ceased to be viable and people moved to the cities, mainly Lisbon and Oporto, and abroad.

This process of different fortunes within countries, and the more general economic strain it represented, were exacerbated by the economic downturns in the early 1990s and, more particularly, from 2008. Youth unemployment rates rose greatly, particularly in Greece, Italy, Portugal and Spain, but also in France.

Migration between countries created more controversy than that within. Yet, migrant workers, such as Portuguese to France and Britain, and Poles to Britain, and Italians to Germany, to cite only some of the more prominent instances, created fewer issues than those posed by cross-cultural migration, such as Algerians to France and Turks to Germany. Even greater sensitivity was attached to migrants fleeing persecution who cannot return home, for example Syrians in the mid-2010s. The problems posed, in truth or fear, by immigrants with very different cultures made the latter category more controversial.

In the 2010s, the rate of immigration from the Middle East and Africa to Europe also became politically highly charged, notably, but not only, with the rise of the Far Right. Indeed, immigration has been one of the major drivers of populism. Some commentators advanced the position that their identity was under threat and adopted a blood-and-soil definition of nationalism. Immigration is likely to increase. The consequences will probably be both benign and malign. Immigration will help counteract the consequences of ageing populations and can be culturally invigorating. At the same time, there are serious pressures on both resources and assumptions, pressures that have encouraged a hostile response from many not on the far right. So, one major element of uncertainty rests on how well this process can, and will, be managed.

THE 'EUROPEAN SPACE'

The issue of the likely future structure of the 'European space' focuses on the future trajectory of the European Union (EU). In Britain, the issue focuses on Brexit, Britain's departure from the EU, which was supported by a referendum in 2016; but it is important to note that in Norway, Switzerland and Russia, Europe contains states that not only are not members of the EU, but also have no intention of joining it. Indeed, the extent to which, when given the vote, many Europeans have voted not to join or to leave the EU, or not to accept closer integration within the EU, is instructive about the continued strength of national identities, as well as indicating the extent of scepticism about the aspirations and achievements of the EU.

President Macron of France's 2018 idea of a multi-speed Europe is significant in this context. However, it is unclear how far this idea, or indeed the EU as a whole, can contain the realities of populism and of the pressures on economies created by a single currency, the Euro, and the related attempt at central direction. More generally, alongside the success of the EU in creating a vast, functioning judicial space, and in acting as an enabler for democratic modernization in southern and eastern Europe from the 1970s and 1990s respectively, its ability to generate solutions is unclear.

GLOBAL ISSUES

Alongside these changes and issues, will come those posed by economic and environmental changes. These are largely global in scale, whether the rise of artificial intelligence or global warming, but all pose challenges to Europe. Global warming is already causing issues in parts of southern Europe, with summer temperatures regularly reaching the mid-40°s centigrade. This warming has been linked to health problems and to summer fires in woodland, as in Greece and Portugal. The omens are not encouraging, not least due to the exposure of Europe to the consequences of population increases and economic growth elsewhere. The declining percentage of the world's wealth and influence in Europe will only make this issue harder to manage.

REDEFINING EUROPE

In the Introduction, Europe was discussed in terms of history, Christendom and geography. At present, the favourite approach among leading commentators is to regard Europe as a value system. This is seen with the Copenhagen criteria, laid down in 1993 as preconditions for countries acceding to the EU, and followed in subsequent accession negotiations including those in the Balkans at present. These criteria include stable political institutions, the guarantee of human rights and the rule of law, economic stability, and an acceptance of EU law. These take precedence over functional systems based on currency (the Eurozone) and border controls (the Schengen zone). Indeed, there are EU members that are not in one or both.

In one respect, this approach to European identity may seem ridiculous. The West German Foreign Minister's claim, in a speech at the United Nations on 27 September 1989, that East Germany risked 'de-Europeanization' if it turned down the opportunity for reform, was absurd as it would not have changed geographically, while the criteria he had in mind had not pertained for most of Europe's history. Moreover, Russia scarcely matches the criteria, while Canada, for example, does in several respects.

Moreover, contrasting ideas about Europe were further focused in the 2000s with the question of Turkish entry to the EU. In practice, the move of Turkey towards increasingly authoritarian methods and Islamic outcomes made such an accession unlikely. It would have taken Europe to the borders of Georgia, Armenia, Iran, Iraq and Syria. Yet that would not have been an outcome different to that of the Roman Empire, or of recent ideas that the Mediterranean is inherently a unit and indeed the root of Europeanness. The reminder of the unfixed nature of Europe's present and of the unpredictable character of its future underlines the inherently controversial question of its identity, and therefore of how best to tell its fascinating and complex history.

A TIMELINE OF EUROPEAN HISTORY

c. 25,000 years ago	*Venus figurines appear in Europe*
10,000 BCE	*Glaciers retreat in Europe*
7000 BCE	*Agriculture spreads to Greece*
4000–2000 BCE	*Causewayed camps and burial chambers appear across Neolithic Europe*
2500 BCE	*Linear A, the first European writing system, appears*
2000 BCE	*First evidence of Minoan civilization in Crete*
c. 1550 BCE	*Mycenae establishes itself as the major power in the Greek peninsula*
1100 BCE	*Fall of Mycenae*
800 BCE	*Phoenician trading base established at Cadiz*
753 BCE	*Legendary foundation of Rome*
499 BCE	*Ionian rebellion marks beginning of Greco-Persian wars*
490 BCE	*Battle of Marathon*
480 BCE	*Battle of Salamis*
431–404 BCE	*Peloponnesian War*
334 BCE	*Alexander the Great invades Asia Minor*
323 BCE	*Death of Alexander the Great*
264–241 BCE	*First Punic War*
260 BCE	*Romans conquer the Etruscans*
218–201 BCE	*Second Punic War*
52 BCE	*Rome conquers Gaul*
44 BCE	*Assassination of Julius Caesar*
9 CE	*Battle of Teutoburg Forest*
117 CE	*Roman empire reaches its greatest extent*
212 CE	*Roman citizenship granted to all free inhabitants of the empire*

312 CE	*Emperor Constantine converts to Christianity*
410	*Visigoths sack Rome*
476	*Last Western Roman Emperor deposed*
507	*Clovis defeats the Visigoths in France*
529	*Benedictine order founded*
711	*Islamic armies invade Spain*
793	*Vikings raid Lindisfarne*
800	*Charlemagne crowned Holy Roman Emperor*
841	*Foundation of Dublin*
843	*Treaty of Verdun*
900	*Establishment of the Kingdom of Alba*
927	*Athelstan unites England*
955	*Battle of Lechfeld*
987	*Hugh Capet establishes the Capetian dynasty in France*
987	*Conversion of Rus to Orthodox Christianity*
1066	*Norman Conquest of England*
1085	*Castile captures Toledo*
1095–99	*First Crusade*
1118	*Foundation of the Knights Templar*
1212	*Battle of Las Navas de Tolosa*
1215	*King John signs the Magna Carta*
1241	*Mongols invade Poland and Hungary*
1314	*Battle of Bannockburn*
1345	*Petrarch discovers Cicero's Letters to Atticus*
1346	*Battle of Crécy*
1348–50	*The Black Death*
1356	*Battle of Poitiers*
1378–1417	*The Great Schism*
1385	*Union of Poland and Lithuania*
1389	*Establishment of Swiss Confederation*
1415	*Battle of Agincourt*
1439	*Gutenberg creates the printing press*
1453	*Ottomans capture Constantinople*

1492	*Columbus reaches West Indies*
1492	*Granada falls to Spain*
1494–1559	*Italian Wars*
1517	*Beginning of Reformation*
1526	*Battle of Mohács*
1529	*Siege of Vienna*
1545–63	*Council of Trent*
1565	*Siege of Malta*
1562–98	*French Wars of Religion*
1571	*Battle of Lepanto*
1588	*Spanish Armada*
1598	*Edict of Nantes*
1568–1648	*Dutch Revolt*
1604–13	*Russia's 'Time of Troubles'*
1618–1648	*Thirty Years' War*
1649	*Charles I is executed*
1683	*Second Siege of Vienna*
1685	*Revocation of the Edict of Nantes*
1687	*Newton publishes the* Principia Mathematica
1688	*Glorious Revolution*
1700–21	*Great Northern War*
1701–14	*War of Spanish Succession*
1712	*Russia's capital moves from Moscow to St Petersburg*
1740–48	*War of Austrian Succession*
1756–63	*Seven Years' War*
1772	*Gustav III seizes greater power in Sweden*
1773–5	*Pugachev Rising*
1773	*Abolition of the Jesuits*
1783	*Annexation of Crimea*
1789	*Start of French Revolution*
1793	*Execution of Louis XVI*
1799	*Napoleon seizes power*
1806	*Dissolution of the Holy Roman Empire*

1815	*Congress of Vienna*
1848	*Revolutions across Europe*
1854–56	*Crimean War*
1861	*Emancipation of the Russian Serfs*
1861	*Kingdom of Italy created*
1870–1	*Franco-Prussian War*
1912–13	*Balkan Wars*
1914–18	*World War I*
1917	*Russian Revolution*
1919	*Versailles Treaty*
1922	*March on Rome*
1929	*Wall Street Crash*
1933	*Hitler becomes Chancellor of Germany*
1936–9	*Spanish Civil War*
1939–45	*World War II*
1949	*Berlin Airlift*
1953	*NATO established*
1955	*Warsaw Pact established*
1956	*Hungarian Revolution*
1961	*Berlin Crisis*
1968	*Prague Spring*
1976	*Death of General Franco*
1989	*Fall of the Berlin Wall*
1991	*Dissolution of the Soviet Union*
1992–95	*Bosnian War*
1999	*Kosovo Crisis*
2008	*Financial Crisis*
2016	*Britain votes to leave the EU*

INDEX

PICTURE CREDITS

Alamy: 80

Bridgeman Images: 49, 72, 88, 168, 186, 191

Metropolitan Museum of Art: 38

State Library of New South Wales: 162

Shutterstock: 27, 30, 34, 40, 42, 55, 145

Wikimedia Commons: 18, 24, 33, 52, 58, 61, 63, 68, 86, 89, 93, 99, 102, 107, 109, 113, 119, 121, 124, 126, 128, 138, 143, 152, 156, 171, 175, 177, 190